ROBERT HEWETT was born in Melbourne in 1949 and is a Drama graduate of Flinders University. For the past ten years he has worked extensively as an actor on stage with the Melbourne Theatre Company, the Nimrod Theatre Sydney, the Tasmanian Theatre Company and J.C. Williamsons; and in film and television.

He began writing in 1980 and his first play *Just ... One Last Dance* received its première that year with the Melbourne Theatre Company. *Gulls* (1983) is his second play and was first performed by the same company.

Robert Hewett lives in Melbourne.

D0898276

Published with the assistance of the Literature Board of the Australia Council.

Bernie Davis as Bill with puppeteer Peter Morris in the National Theatre Company production at the Greenroom, Perth, 1983, directed by Edgar Metcalfe, designed by Sally-Ann Parsons. Photo by Geoff Lovell.

Gulls

Robert Hewett

CURRENCY PRESS · SYDNEY

CURRENCY PLAYS
General Editor: Katharine Brisbane

First published in 1984 by
Currency Press Pty Ltd,
PO Box 452 Paddington,
N.S.W. 2021, Australia

National Library of Australia card number
and ISBN 0 86819 085 3

Typeset by Saba Graphics Ltd, Christchurch, New Zealand
Printed by Colorcraft, Hong Kong

Author's Note

I was a boy of fifteen visiting an 'institution' to operate the spinning wheel at its annual fete. Each patient had been given twelve pennies to spend. One lady spent her entire allotment at the wheel but didn't win a prize. She became extremely upset, as did I, in trying to explain that her number had not come up. A large group of patients gathered and consoled her as she started to cry. I gave her back some pennies until she won a prize.

Sixteen years later I had cause again to visit a neighbouring 'institution'. The feeling of the place hadn't changed at all. It was stiflingly warm inside. Many patients were sitting watching television, or asleep. A person was moving about dispensing tablets and small wax paper cups of water. It was mid-afternoon. As I was let out, an elderly gentleman smiled at me and tried to speak. Again I couldn't understand. Finally in desperation he held up his nicotine-stained fingers, and I saw the remnants of a roll-your-own cigarette, stuck to a large mound of burnt flesh on his forefinger. He pulled it off, took the cigarette I offered and left. So did I.

From these experiences, and others, emerged an idea.

The first submittable draft of *Gulls* was handed to the Melbourne Theatre Company in February 1982, and subsequently given a Sunday reading. Over the next few weeks I re-wrote considerably, and by chance ran into Bruce Myles in the street, haranguing him about the text all the way to a Schoolsday of the current Shakespeare programme. We agreed to meet and discuss the new draft, after which he decided to come in on the project. Throughout the mid year more research was done, more rewrites, and clarification of the text — a continual process of elimination, explanation and development.

Finally we had the script in a state where we thought a quick read through by the actors would be beneficial. They gathered one night at my home and we slowly worked through the text — stopping whenever there was a contentious issue, discussing what we had been trying to do at that point, and the actor telling us what he or she thought. Often it was merely a rearrangement of words — sometimes a redefinition of intention. Suddenly it was early morning and they dispersed. Bruce and I continued for another hour, looking at areas we thought would benefit from further development. He was moving into rehearsal shortly, and I had other work on my plate, so the project was laid to rest until early January when we would workshop for a week.

The workshop was open slather — a no-holds-barred wrestling match between actors and text, with Myles as referee. Midway through we had sorted out most of the characters' dilemmas, but in doing so had neglected, or rather confused the protagonist's journey. The problem stemmed from the disjointed time sequences which had become muddied. After the final readthrough and discussion on the Friday I again worked through the text from Bill's point of view, mindful of his problem. Once this was solved most of everything else seemed to fall into place.

We were now only a week away from rehearsal, so our concentration had to move to the puppets — an integral part of the action and theme. Working with the puppeteers, puppet maker and designer, we had to strike a balance between design requirements and practicability. From initial conflict we worked the balance down to three basic requirements — wing movement, wing closure and body mobility. The operator's body movement was to add as much to the illusion as the puppet itself.

The end result is what you see. I cannot stress enough the benefit of the workshop process, nor the enormous input of the director in getting it to this stage. However, I truly believe it should not be an exceptional circumstance for any new play, but the norm.

Director's Note

Bruce Myles

Firstly, I would like to say that I think it is vital for our playwrights to view the State theatre companies as resource centres for the development of their work. The process that *Gulls* underwent towards the initial production at the Melbourne Theatre Company took almost a year and stands a good example of the way the resources of a large company can be effectively used in the service of a developing playwright.

Robert Hewett submitted the script to the MTC where it was given a written assessment by the literary adviser, Ray Lawler, who then discussed the play with the author.

At this point a public reading was set up in the MTC series of Monthly Readings for Playwrights. This is a valuable stage for the writer: the play can now be shared with other people. He or she can begin to assess whether their ideas are coming across in the way intended. During the short rehearsal period there is opportunity for the actors to share their impression of the roles with the playwright; and after the reading the audience is invited to discuss the play with writer and cast.

It was at the Sunday reading that I caught up with the play. I was impressed by the structure of the piece; and even more by the central character who communicated beautifully to the audience. The theme was one that particularly interested me, especially in the inventive and theatrical way Robert was exploring it.

Following the reading he and I discussed our own responses and those of the audience and agreed on areas where more work needed to be done. By that time I was very keen to do the play at the Russell Street Theatre. We persuaded the Repertoire Committee and production dates were settled far enough ahead for us to work together on the script in order to realise the full potential we now saw for it.

Now we set about examining the play, slowly and in enormous detail, clarifying the themes and consolidating the points of view the author wanted to express. Every scene, every moment was discussed in length. Gradually he was giving more dimension to his characters, the storyline was getting tighter and the momentum of the play began to flow smoothly in the right direction.

It was during this period that *Gulls* was cast, and when Robert had completed work on the new draft we called the cast together for a reading. Hearing the play again after weeks of dismantling gave us a fresh perspective. The actors, too, were now beginning to investigate their roles and were able to ask many questions and make many suggestions for us to consider when putting the next draft together for the workshop period prior to rehearsals.

The workshop was a passionate, demanding, stimulating week. The contribution from the cast was tremendous. The pressure on Robert to be clear and precise, and alert to the unexpected idea which could bring a fresh dimension to a character was enormous. Every question, every doubt was thrashed out honestly and in detail. By the time the rehearsal period was due we shared a common understanding of what the play was about.

Up to this point our main consideration had been to get the text right. Now it was time to concentrate on the puppets — an integral part of the action and theme. A week was spent prior to rehearsal with the puppeteers, puppet maker and designer, fitting this vital element into the play.

By the time rehearsals started, nearly twelve months after the script was first submitted, we felt ready to tackle the play with confidence. Until now the focus had been on the writer and his script; now it was time to interpret the play, to bring to it our own perceptions, make our own choices and mould our own individual production. It was a very imaginative, positive rehearsal period, and I am quite certain that the quality achieved was due in no small way to the many weeks of thorough, detailed and thoughtful work done in advance.

Gulls is a play which confronts its audience both in subject matter and style. Critics in Melbourne greeted it as 'an unlikely play' and 'strikingly beautiful'. Leonard Radic in the *Age* (3 March 1983) wrote: '*Gulls* is a moving, compassionate play on the theme of impairment. You would have to be stony-hearted not to be stirred by it.' And Samela Harris in Adelaide admitted *(Australian* 29 September) 'This steely critic was twice reduced to tears.' Mardy Amos in Perth *(Australian* 29 July) described it as 'a richly humorous, perceptive and deeply moving play which treads a fine line away from the bathos it could have slipped into had it been miscast'.

In reviewing the original Melbourne production, Laurie Landray (*Herald*, 3 March 1983) described Simon Chilvers' Bill as '. . . totally in command of an immensely difficult role that calls for childlike simplicity, the illumined wonder of his rapport with seagulls on the beach, intensely moving speechless rage, and the urbane wit of his alter ego.'' The theatrical device of the puppets succeeded in illuminating ideas with utter simplicity; words could not have been as effective. Most of the critics described the gulls as the embodiment of freedom. 'The device is curiously effective', wrote Radic, 'primarily because the swooping, soaring birds serve to point up even more Billy's acute sense of isolation. With the gulls he can communicate, albeit at a primitive level.'

Gulls will have many more productions and many more interpretations. Looking back over my own response to the first year of its life I felt that we had given an ambitious new play every possibility of succeeding.

Melbourne 1983

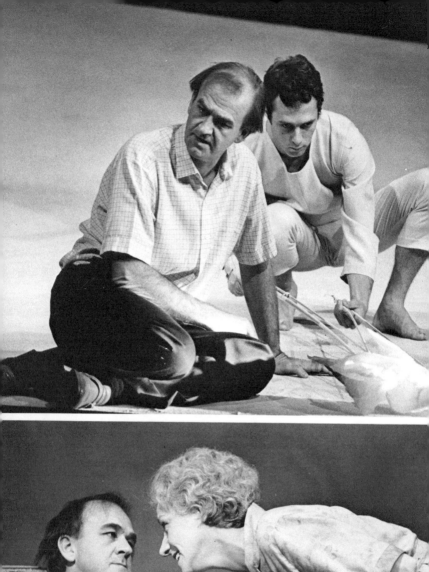

The Melbourne Theatre Company production. Above left: Simon Chilvers as Bill with puppeteer Ian Cuming. Left: Simon Chilvers with Monica Maughan as Molly. Above: Monica Maughan, Simon Chilvers, Ian Cuming and Bruno Annetta. Photos by David Parker.

The Stage Company production, Space Theatre, Adelaide, 1983, directed by Don Gay and designed by Peter Mumford.
Left: Barbara West as Molly and Don Barker as Bill.
Above: Anna Pike as Frances with Don Barker and puppeteers Richard Margetson and Russell Garbutt.
Photos by Peter Mumford.

Frances and Bill. Above: Jenny McNae and Bernie Davis in Perth. Below: Babs McMillan and Simon Chilvers in Melbourne. Photos by Geoff Lovell and David Parker.

GULLS

Bernie Davis with Margaret Anketell as Molly in the Perth production. Photo by Geoff Lovell.

Gulls was first performed by the Melbourne Theatre Company at the Russell Street Theatre on 1 March 1983 with the following cast:

BILL CLEMENTS	Simon Chilvers
FRANCES CLEMENTS	Babs McMillan
MOLLY DWYER	Monica Maughan
DAN	Robert Essex
Puppeteers	Ian Cuming
	Bruno Annetta

Designed by Kim Carpenter
Lighting Design by Jamie Lewis
Music by Martin Friedel
Puppets directed by Robert Hewett
Directed by Bruce Myles

CHARACTERS

BILL CLEMENTS, about forty years old
FRANCES, his sister, in her mid-thirties
MOLLY DWYER, a neighbour, in her mid-sixties
DAN, the same age as Bill
Two seagulls

AUTHOR'S NOTE

The two gulls are rod-operated puppets. The operators should use stylised movement and dress. The gulls should be larger than life but not overly so; and be set on poles of reasonable length or extendable so that they may fly over the audience. They should have operable wings and be virtually featureless.

SETTING

A house and adjacent beach at Portarlington. The time is the present and the action takes place over a period of eighteen months. The main acting areas are the living room of Frances' house, her brother Bill's bedroom and the beach front. The house is sparsely furnished and the overall effect is of slight decay. There is a front and back verandah and a single washing line running down one side. The back door leads onto the verandah, which in turn leads down to the beach (the forestage). A dune rises behind the house.

ACT ONE

A wind chime is heard and then the strains of a harmonica as from the back of the house two gulls rise and circle before coming down either side of the house to the forestage. They swoop to either side and hover there as the lights on the living area rise. BILL *and* DAN *are sitting at the table drinking sherry —* BILL *has hardly touched his. He is dressed in pyjamas and jumper.* DAN *wears a suit, slightly crumpled from having spent the day in the car.* BILL *stands and moves to the front of the living area: the gulls swoop and fly off either side.* DAN *refills his glass.*

DAN: It'll come to me in a minute . . . he had chalk marks round his fly, from pulling his pants up, and his gut hung out so far they never stayed there for long — what was his name?

BILL: Chalk marks?

DAN: He took us for double geography — had to really battle to keep awake, keep your head off the desk. Oh, what was his name?

BILL: Mumbles.

DAN: Mumbles, that was it. He'd have half the class out on the oval, lining — no, what do you call it?

BILL: Marking.

DAN: Marking, marking the oval. [*Imitating the master*] 'In preparation for the house athletics trials the more iiiiiintelligent boyce can have a pppractical demonstration in soil conservation and mark up the oval. Volunteers?

[*He looks about. No one is obviously volunteering*] 'Williams and Ryecroft, you look eeeager to me. The rest of you can stop slinking behind your desks and rrread Chapter Four on "The Alluvial Plains of Italy". One word out of you, Clements, and it's straight to the head.' Remember?

BILL: I don't recall it.

DAN: Soon as he was out the door all hell'd break loose. That fat kid, you know, ate banana sandwiches that had gone brown, soon as Mumbles was out the door we hurled him in the geography cupboard and locked the door.

BILL: Bagley. It was Bagley we locked in the geography library.

DAN: Who was the one we railroaded into that cupboard? There was Williams and Ryecroft down the front, you and me and Bagley over by the window. [*Looking to* BILL] Was it Bagley we locked in the cupboard?

BILL: People like Bagley aren't meant to grow old. It's a good thing they go early; they would never have lasted the distance. What chance did he ever have? Sitting there by himself. His only contact with humanity the odd poke in the back with a ruler.

DAN: Mumbles eh . . . What on earth happened to Mumbles?

BILL: Bagley could never get over the vaulting horse. Endless instructors made him go back, in front of the entire class, 'Make a decent effort, Bagley'. And this huge blubbery whale would lurch into flight, be marooned on top, then come crashing to the mat below. Jeered at. The laughing stock of the class. No wonder he killed himself.

DAN: S'pose he's retired now.

BILL: Even the gesture was wasted. Nobody missed him.

DAN: We'd be out on the oval marking up for a week beforehand.

BILL: Bagley was something that dragged the class average down. There was never any question as to why this should be so. That there could be something scaring the shit out of him. One less in the class to worry about. Allowed the averages to increase. Never questioning their motives — or his. Better out of it. That death was quicker and less painful than the one he would have faced if he had survived.

DAN: You were the only one who had their head screwed

on the right way. The right attitude. I was envious of
you then.

BILL: We were cruel bastards to Bagley.

DAN: They never had any power over you, Billy. You had
it in perspective, and it rattled them. Never the most
important thing it was to them or us. It scared them,
Billy. They respected you for that, so did I.

BILL: You place an importance on something that
was never there.

DAN: You must have been aware of it. God, I can still see
Mumbles' face. Red with contained rage. He never gave
in. Trying to break you down. Baiting you, catch you
out. Every time he tackled you he failed. You always
had the answer. And every time he failed he exposed
his own basic weakness. [*Smiling to* BILL] He hated
you for that.

BILL: You're talking crap.

[*He stands and walks toward the audience and
addresses them directly.*]

I don't understand much of what this man is talking
about. He in fact is doing the talking. He's talking to
himself. I don't remember or wish to remember what he
is talking about. He is talking of another life.

DAN: What's the matter, Billy, you're not drinking much?

BILL: Drinking. He'd been drinking.

DAN: Want some more?

BILL: It was Friday afternoon. House athletic trials.

DAN: You know what? I reckon Mumbles is probably still
shoving the same old garbage down the throats of
unsuspecting school kids.

BILL: I found a bottle of gin. Empty. Stuffed into the top
of a garbage bin, behind the grandstand. You were
still changing.

DAN: He would have given his right arm to catch you out.
Just once.

BILL: A thud on my shoulder almost knocked the bottle
from my hand. I was spun about. It was Mumbles. His
fingers digging into my shoulders. Yelling at me.
Didn't stop to ask if the bottle was mine or not. Just

starting yelling. You were changing and had just come out of the shed.

DAN: Remember he'd perve around the corner of the changing shed. Trying to catch us smoking was his excuse.

BILL: All those veins across his cheeks and nose, filling with blood. His face was screaming at me and all I kept looking at was this map of the world on his face. He sniffed the bottle, then held it up in the air. Triumphant. Grabbing my hair he pulled me around the front of the grandstand. Paraded me victoriously before the entire school and parents watching the trials. I looked back for you, and you were bent double, pissing yourself with laughter, clutching your sandshoes.

DAN: Looking back on it, I suppose he wasn't such a bad old stick.

BILL: He hurled me through the office door. Then someone came in, whispered, and he left. The corridor filled with voices. Hushed. Something had happened. I was forgotten about. Stood for hours. Five o'clock. Stuck my head outside. No one. They'd all gone home. I fled the office. Grabbed my bag. A pencil case spilt its contents. I didn't stop. I tore, raced, ran breathless to the station. As I came through the gate I could see a group of people standing up the other end. I walked closer and recognised a few of the teachers. I froze. Mumbles was standing in the centre waving his arms about. He turned. Screamed at me. I've never seen such a look of hate. His face was about to crack open. I couldn't understand what he was talking about. Someone ran and told me to go to the next station along and catch the train home. I turned to go and caught sight of a school uniform being put into a bag. Then I realised it was only a sleeve, and it had an arm sticking out of it. It was Bagley. Mumbles was screaming at me. He would see me in the morning in his office. But I couldn't move. I just kept staring at these bits of clothing they were shoving in the bag. That night we both got drunk. That was the night . . .

DAN: What do you mean by those strange sounds? Do you understand what I'm saying? Reckon I might as well talk to a brick wall.

BILL: We'd taken three books out of the geography library. Identical books. All in his name. *Deserts of the World*, Antony Bagley. *Deserts of the World*, Antony Bagley.

DAN: Will you stop babbling.

BILL: Three copies.

DAN: Sit down, Billy, come on.

BILL: We shoved them up the other end of the shelves near the W's. He must have found them and put them in his bag.

DAN: I can't understand. Calm down.

BILL: They were sprawled all over the track. Someone had taken notice of him.

DAN: Come on, mate, take it easy.

BILL: Oh God, I've wet myself. Frances is going to be so angry.

[*He goes back and sits down.* DAN *stares at him. They settle.*]

DAN: You know, kid, you've got it made here. Nothing to do but sit around all day, waited on hand and foot; it's a dog's life, eh? You're sitting pretty and don't even know it.

BILL: When you have all the time in the world it's frightening what you can uncover. He must have been able to see all that way. That's what frightened the shit out of Antony Bagley.

[FRANCES *approaches the house carrying a box of groceries. She pauses momentarily, looking back at* DAN's *car, then enters the house.*]

BILL: My sister, Frances.

FRANCES: I wondered if we were going to see you again.

[DAN *rises to greet her*]

How are you, Dan?

DAN: Let myself in, hope you don't mind.

FRANCES: No, 'course not. Bit of company for him.

DAN: Yeah.

FRANCES: It's been months.

DAN: I was working in the district, thought I might as well pop in, see how the kid's getting on.

FRANCES: Don't call him that.

DAN: Just a turn of phrase.

[*A slightly awkward pause until* FRANCES *decides to put away the groceries.*]

DAN: House is looking better than the last time.

FRANCES: The other time.

DAN: Yes . . . Looking better.

FRANCES: Haven't done anything to it, have we, sport? You made yourself a cup of anything?

DAN: Helped ourselves to a glass of sherry.

[*She removes* BILL'*s untouched glass.*]

FRANCES: Not for him. You know better than that, Billy. You want something to eat?

[BILL *shakes his head.*]

Fill up the jug then.

[*He remains seated.*]

What's the matter with you, cat got your tongue?

DAN: He's been babbling on for hours, couldn't stop him. He's put on a bit of weight, Frances.

[*She goes and fills the jug.*]

FRANCES: I can't give him much exercise, and he won't budge from in front of that television set.

DAN: Oh, yeah.

FRANCES: It's my Billy sitter. Got it with money left over from the sale of the other place.

DAN: Can I put anything away?

FRANCES: No, I'm right.

[*She smiles and walks past him to where* BILL *is seated.*]

How are you, Billy, have a nice chat to Dan? What's the matter with you, sport?

[BILL *places his hands over his lap and turns away.*]

Have you wet yourself, Billy?

[*She shoves her hand inside his pyjamas.*]

DAN: He went to the dunny about half an hour ago.

FRANCES: What have you done, then? Didn't you aim right?

You're a grub at times, Billy, you know that, don't you? You can understand well enough what I'm talking about, can't you?

[BILL *shakes his head, no.*]

Oh really, I didn't come down in the last shower, you know. Was there something really interesting on the telly, eh? Couldn't wait to get back to watch it?

DAN: Telly wasn't on.

FRANCES: [*going off to make the coffee*] Well, you've just been a lazy bones then, haven't you? You can stay wet till I've had my tea and Dan's gone. And you needn't sulk, it serves yourself right. [*Re-entering with the coffee*] Black, one sugar, right?

DAN: Right.

FRANCES: [*sitting down*] How's Elizabeth?

DAN: Expecting.

FRANCES: So I heard.

DAN: Oh.

FRANCES: Can't remember who told me.

DAN: Beginning to show. Only four months to go now.

FRANCES: That's flown.

DAN: She doesn't think so.

[*He sips his coffee. It's too hot.*]

DAN: If it's a boy we thought we might call him Billy.

FRANCES: Oh.

DAN: You're still looking a hundred per cent, Frances.

FRANCES: Thanks to the move down here. I knew I made the right decision. For both of us.

DAN: He's got some red blotches round his neck and face. They anything to worry about?

FRANCES: Mossie bites. We put our fist through the fly screen the other night, didn't we, sport?

DAN: Bit of a temper.

FRANCES: Haven't a clue what it was all about. Saw a bird or something and tried to catch it.

DAN: He and I used to go bird catching when we were kids. In the vacant block next to your Mum and Dad's. Never caught a single bloody one. Remember?

FRANCES: No. Why do you want to call your son Bill?

DAN: Oh, it's only a gesture. You know.

FRANCES: I see.

DAN: You don't like the idea?

FRANCES: Call it what you want. [*Getting up*] Sure I can't fix you some food?

DAN: Nah, got to hit the road. No rest for the wicked.
    [*He moves to kiss her. She turns away.*]

DAN: Not often I get down this way. Usually covered by the country boys.
    [*He picks up his bag and makes to leave.*]
    Does he still like lolly bars?

FRANCES: Yes, but he shouldn't eat too many.

DAN: Oh right, the weight.
    [*He takes several samples from his bag.*]
    It's a new line we're flogging, they're not bad. Well, look after yourself. [*Going over to* BILL] See you later, Billy. Nice talking to you. Look after Frances, won't you? See you soon.

FRANCES: Next time let us know when you're coming.

DAN: Yeah.

FRANCES: Make it a lunchtime and I'll have something for you.

DAN: Will do.
    [*He moves toward her. She lowers her head, but this time he kisses her lightly on the forehead.*]

FRANCES: Nice to see you again. [*Looking up at him*] Give my regards to Elizabeth. [*Moving out ahead of him*] I'll see you to the car.

DAN: Bye, Billy.
    [*He exits after her.* BILL *stands, walks to the door and looks after them. He walks over to the table where the chocolate bars are, partially unwraps one, places another in his pocket and walks down to the audience, munching.*]

BILL: Not bad, not too bad at all. She's right, though. If I eat too many I'll get really fat. What the hell. [*Eating more*] You see, I'm not all here. Simplest way of putting it. Pardon me. [*Dislodging a piece of caramel stuck in his mouth*] Opinions vary from early teens and plummet

rapidly from there. Dr Andrews, our local GP, reckons
about seven or eight. But that's what I reckon about him
too. You can't sit for about a week after one of his
injections.

[*He eats more lolly bar.*]

That was a turn up for the books. At that stage we hadn't
seen Dan for about six months. He was the only one out
of the class that still visited me. Well, it wasn't me he was
calling round to see, but I didn't cotton on to that then.
Oh, I knew he'd always had the hots for Frances ever
since she started to develop, but she wasn't interested.
Dan and I settled for jerking off over an old copy of *Man*
magazine. You know, blonde ladies chatting to one
another, crossed legs, and a beach ball stuck in their laps.
Frances is going to come marching back in a minute and
try and change me. I knew I shouldn't have weed my
pyjamas but I was a bit — over excited. I don't — can't
remember most of what Dan talked about. Only every
now and then does this old brain rev up its engines, and
then I understand, and remember. So much. But there is
no beginning — only, before then, since then, here,
sitting on the beach, up at the house she'd bought for me
— us. And when I remember, I think: Time's up! Here
comes Frances. If she finds me with this I won't get any
dinner. Here, catch. [*Tossing it into the audience*] Finish
it off, it's not too bad.

[*He moves back to the house and is about to enter.*]

Oh, one more thing, at the end of tonight I'm going to
slash my throat from ear to ear.

[BILL *dashes in, turns on the television and sits as*
FRANCES *enters from the front of the house.*]

FRANCES: Well, well, fancy that.

[*She clears away his cup and moves off into the
kitchen.*]

How many of those lolly bars did you manage to scoff
down your face?

BILL: [*to the audience*] Not a word.

[*She re-enters and walks over to him and takes one
out of his pocket.*]

FRANCES: Put it back, you can have one after dinner.

   [*He places it back on the table.*]

   You brought the washing in?

   [*He walks back to his seat.*]

   Okay, sport, off with the TV and bring the washing in.
   No *Bugs Bunny* till you've done your chores.

BILL: *Bugs Bunny* is not my favourite TV programme.
   Frances thinks it is, though, so we watch it, religiously.

FRANCES: Don't think you can fool me with any of your
   old tricks. I know perfectly well you can understand
   me. Go on, out and bring the washing in.

   [*He remains seated.*]

   It'll be straight to bed in your wet pyjamas, no TV, no
   dinner, no nothing. You've got to pull your weight
   about the place too.

   [*Reluctantly he gets up and moves to the outside
   area.* FRANCES *continues to put things away and
   prepare the evening meal.*]

BILL: It's very hard to pull the wool over Frances' eyes,
   she's a wake-up to everything I do — just about, anyway.

   [*He takes a lolly bar out of his pocket.*]

FRANCES: Basket's sitting where you left it. How's Mrs
   Dwyer?

BILL: Mrs Dwyer lives two down. She had a family but
   they all grew up and left home. She makes sure I have
   lunch when Frances is at work.

FRANCES: Her arthritis any better?

BILL: Mrs Dwyer also suffers from every disease known to
   man. If you ever bump into her she'll only be too
   willing to bore the pants off you with her entire medi-
   cal history.

FRANCES: Most unlike Dan to call in unannounced,
   wasn't it?

BILL: Why did she say that? We were talking about Mrs
   Dwyer.

FRANCES: Mrs Dwyer see Dr Andrews today?

BILL: She uses the same doctor as me. He's a highly
   specialised person.

FRANCES: Last time she went he gave her a new prescription. Did she find the new prescription worked any better? That's good.

BILL: These one-sided conversations are fascinating. Ever listen to a person talking to a dog, or a small child? You don't have to do a thing. They answer every question they put to you. As long as you smile or wag your tail, they have a ball.

[*He finishes the washing and brings it inside.*]

Sometimes they even reward you with small gifts. Chocolate bars and comics happen to be my favourite.

FRANCES: Now that wasn't such a big effort, was it? Leave them on the table, we'll fold them after.

[*He remains standing.*]

Here, you shell the peas while you watch TV.

[*She hands him a colander and saucepan and turns the television on.*]

There's still a bit of *Bugs Bunny* on.

[*He remains standing next to the washing basket. For the first time he speaks directly to* FRANCES *in a completely different vocal tone to that in which he has been addressing the audience. He is barely audible and impossible to understand. What he is trying to say is 'You forgot to change my pants', the only word coming out is a conglomerate of pants — 'Aapaa'. Each time he repeats the word he becomes vocally stronger.*]

Oh, sport, I'm sorry. Come here.

[*She sorts through the washing and gets out a clean pair of pyjamas.*]

We need to get a couple of new pairs, these have almost had it. Here you go.

[*She takes down his pyjama pants.*]

BILL: I'd talk amongst yourselves for a while, this isn't a pretty sight.

FRANCES: Did we get over-excited when Dan was here? Oh, Billy, I thought we were past this stage.

[FRANCES *throws them in the bin.*]

BILL: So did I.

FRANCES: [*seeing* BILL *struggling with his jumper*] What are you doing?

[*She can't help laughing.*]

BILL: Trying to maintain some dignity.

FRANCES: Hold still. [*Releasing him from the jumper*] There you go. Nice to see Dan, wasn't it?

[BILL *has difficulty putting his legs in the pyjamas.*] No, sport, you're putting them on back to front.

BILL: This is an old trick. I do it when I want to get out of boring chores like shelling the peas.

FRANCES: Here we go. [*Swivelling the pyjamas around the right way*] That's it, lift your leg and in we go. Now the other, and jump.

[*He does so and* FRANCES *pulls them up around his waist.*]

You can tie the knot, you're not that useless.

[*She puts on the dressing-gown and goes back to preparing the evening meal.*]

BILL: Well, that killed five minutes, didn't it?

FRANCES: In the morning we'll go down to Woolworths and get you a couple of new pairs.

BILL: Woolworths is my favourite store. We rarely shop anywhere else. The cashier lady usually gives me a Mars bar or something. I think she fancies me, actually.

FRANCES: What did you and Dan talk about? School?

BILL: We rarely talk about anything else. The past. That's all we had in common. I think he feels a bit guilty about me. It was pure luck that he isn't in the same boat, or dead. Fluke of nature.

FRANCES: You remember school?

BILL: No, he remembers school. At times I can't remember what I did five minutes ago, let alone things that happened twenty years in the past.

FRANCES: Christ, these shoes are killing me.

[*She kicks them off.*]

BILL: Frances works in the library. Two days a week all day, Tuesdays and Thursdays, half days. It supplements my pension cheque. When Mum died, Frances inherited me. Most people usually get money, or heirlooms and such stuff. Frances really dipped out. She could do something better than helping out in a library, but she's the only one left to take care of me. I love her for that. She's given up quite a bit for me, Frances has.

FRANCES: Library was swarming with school kids today, all wanting special project material. Bloody teachers hadn't rung up and warned us they were coming. Only Jan and me on, too.

BILL: I like Jan. She works with Frances. I like her mainly because of her sweet nature and big knockers. I felt them once. They're real, too. Huge. She hit me.

FRANCES: How are you going with the peas, sport?

[*She comes over to where* BILL *is sitting.*]

Oh, come on, you can do better than that. What's the matter with you today? I'm not in the mood for any of your shenanigans, had enough of that at the library. Here, I'll help you.

[*He knocks over the colander of peas as she sits to help.*]

What did you do that for?

[*He looks away.*]

Look at me, sport. What's the matter with you? Pick them up. Go on, pick them up.

[BILL *walks over to the TV and turns it up.*]

OK, no TV until you pick up all the peas.

[*She turns it off. He sits defiantly in the chair.*]

Get down on the floor and pick them up.

[*He leans over, picks one up, opens it and eats the contents.*]

You do it on purpose, Billy, you do it on purpose.

[*He reaches for another pea and she grabs his hand.* BILL *knocks her hand away and begins to shell it.*]

If you put that near your mouth it's no TV for a week. You understand that, don't you?

[*He shells the pea directly onto the floor.*]

Pick up the rest of the peas. Billy, I'm warning you.

[*He treads the pea into the ground.*]

You'll push your luck too far, in a minute.

[*He raises his foot and stamps it down onto the peas on the floor.*]

You've asked for it, Billy.

[*She grabs hold of him and slaps him around the legs.*]

I won't take any more of your nonsense.

[*He holds her away.*]

Take your hand off me. Billy.

[*He doesn't.*]

I'm warning you, take . . . your hand, off me.

[*He doesn't.*]

Right, you —

[*She knocks his hand off and slaps him across the face. He knocks her to the floor and emits a loud cry.* FRANCES *remains on the floor, thinks for a moment, collects herself together, and rises.*]

OK, sport, we knew what would happen if this sort of behaviour occurred again. It's out. You know I can't control you when you have this sort of mood on. All I asked you to do was shell the peas. That's all. I know you can understand me. Dr Andrews said so, and you know so, Billy — you know when you're doing wrong. I don't want to, but I'll have to send you back to the hostel.

[BILL *looks up.*]

BILL: I remember this place . . .

FRANCES: I can't control you when you turn on me, Billy . . .

BILL: . . . the corner bed, in a temporary building that had stayed, like me, for several years, forgotten.

FRANCES: I can't. I thought we understood one another from the last time . . .

BILL: Forgotten . . .

FRANCES: Your strength could knock me out . . .

BILL: . . . forgotten, until one day . . .

FRANCES: You do understand me . . .

BILL: . . . One day, a face . . .

FRANCES: please underst —

BILL: . . . a face familiar to me appeared at the door.

FRANCES: Please understand me.

BILL: It was Frances.

[*He begins to cry.*]

FRANCES: Don't cry, sport, don't cry . . .

[*She walks over to him and puts her arms around him.*]

Come on, look at me. We'll give it another go, come on.

[*She goes to pick up the peas. He turns to the audience.*]

BILL: When I was in my final year at school I was in an accident. It was the night Bagley went. Dan and I; guilty; drunk. Dan, who was driving, walked away. I died. My body regained consciousness after several minutes. My brain, however, did not. Together we're imprisoned by a world that condemns us to the life of some three-year old going on forty.

[*The voice of* MOLLY DWYER *can be heard.*]

MOLLY: Cooee, you in, Frances?

BILL: Mrs Dwyer. Her timing is perfect.

FRANCES: Oh Christ, no.

MOLLY: [*peering through the fly wire door*] You in, Frances? Hallo, Billy. Frances home yet?

FRANCES: I'm down here, Molly.

MOLLY: Had an accident with the peas?

FRANCES: Sort of.

MOLLY: Didn't eat much of his lunch today, did you, Billy, eh? You right, Frances?

[*She goes to help her.*]

BILL: Would you eat fish paste sandwiches on yesterday's bread?

MOLLY: Normally eats all his sandwiches. Here, you've left one.

[*She bends down and picks up a pea.*]

BILL: Mrs Dwyer loves fish paste. I skip lunch on those days. Mrs Dwyer, on the other hand, has a passion for paste of any kind. They make me want to throw up.

MOLLY: Those tablets Bob Andrews gave me were bloody useless. The arthritis is worse than ever.

FRANCES: Oh, Molly, that's too bad.

MOLLY: You know, I woke up this morning, didn't sleep at all well last night, I woke up this morning and my hand was lying next to me like a claw. Don't know if I'll be able to make practice this week.

BILL: Mrs Dwyer's other passion beside fish paste is bowls.

FRANCES: Will they be able to field a team without you?

MOLLY: Mrs Baldock in Henrietta Street usually gets a guernsey, she's not up to tournament standard, though. Not that I'm saying she's bad, but she's not up to tournament standard. She hurls the ball. Blessed hand.

FRANCES: We're having chops for dinner, care to join us?

BILL: She's already eaten. Eats at four o'clock, so it's quite safe to ask her.

MOLLY: I've already eaten, Frances, thanks all the same. Some other time, maybe.

FRANCES: Anytime, Molly, the house is always open to you.

BILL: Sunday's usually the day. Frances always cooks a roast for us on Sunday, and Mrs Dwyer usually has to call in just about the time we're going to sit down.

MOLLY: And what's our boy been up to? You're a bit down in the mouth.

FRANCES: He's been in a foul mood ever since I got in.

MOLLY: What happened? He was right as rain an hour ago. Would it have anything to do with those peas being on the floor?

FRANCES: Just a little.

MOLLY: You been upsetting your sister Frances have you, Billy? You been a bad boy? You should look after your sister Frances, she's one in a million. You're lucky to have her. What have you been eating? Chocolate.

[*She takes out her handkerchief, spits on it, and wipes his mouth.*]

You're a little grub at times, you know that, don't you? [*Pinching his cheek*] You should behave yourself for your sister. She's got to work all day down the library to keep you in house and home. Now give us a big kiss before I go, eh?

[BILLY *looks at the floor.*]

You getting shy on your Aunty Molly? Who's me favourite boy then, eh? Give us a bye-bye kiss.

BILL: I hate this bit.

MOLLY: Come on, Billy, a nigh-nigh kiss for your Aunty Molly.

[BILLY *dribbles.*]

Oh, what are you dribbling for? Can't you wait for your tea? Here.

[*She takes the handkerchief out of her pocket and wipes his mouth.*]

BILL: Usually works.

MOLLY: What are you trying to say? You hungry for your tea?

FRANCES: Say good night to Mrs Dwyer and thank her for lunch.

[BILL *attempts to say 'good night'.*]

MOLLY: And the same to you with brass knobs on. Shake hands then if you won't kiss me. Y'think you're too big to kiss your Aunty Molly, that it?

[*She picks up his hand and shakes it.*]

Good night, Billy, see you tomorrow for lunch.

FRANCES: Was there something you wanted, Molly?

BILL: Usually not. She's just lonely.

MOLLY: Bugger, you got any Lux? Uniform's really pitiful and I'm clean out.

FRANCES: Sure, in the laundry.

[*They both exit.*]

BILL: On the day we moved down here Mrs Dwyer was the first to make herself known. We'd only been here an hour! I was told to sit and not move. So I did. I couldn't believe it. This was it and a bit. Frances said so. The sea air, a new house, and it was cheaper too. She didn't want to move into the old place after Mum died. Wouldn't have a bar of it. Didn't worry me. She threw most of the furniture away. Good oh! 'We'll just keep the bare essentials', she said. I kept wondering when the new stuff would arrive. It never did. Didn't understand

why. (Not then, anyway.) Frances was out the back
unloading the car, and I was sitting at this table, not
moving, when Mrs Dwyer burst through the door with
a flummery.

MOLLY: [*giving a perfunctory knock before walking in*]
Cooee, anybody in?

[BILLY *stands, slightly alarmed at the intruder.*]

Hallo, Molly Dwyer's the name, don't get up, I live two
down. Welcome to the neighbourhood. [*Holding out
the flummery*] Made you this for dessert. I know what
it's like when you're in the middle of shifting, can't
put your hands on anything, and you never have a
chance to think of dessert. Do you like flummery?

[BILL *takes the bowl.*]

I saw them take the sign down and I've been wondering
when you were going to shift in.

[BILL *puts a finger in the bowl to taste it but before
he can put it to his mouth* MOLLY *speaks.*]

It's strawberry. I hope you like strawberry. Where's
your wife got to? I saw her before unloading the car.

[BILL *looks incredulously at her then licks his finger
as an afterthought.*]

You've bought a nice house here, hope you don't mind
me asking. How much did you pay?

[BILL *is delighted with it and sits.*]

No, you're quite right. It was rude of me to even bring
it up. You'll be pleased to know this area has really
gone ahead in the last few years. They're building a
Woolworths. [*Confiding in* BILL] That'll be a bit of
competition for George Williams, won't be able to
palm his stale stock off on you now. [*Prodding him
with her finger*] You bought at the right time.

[BILL *smiles at her.*]

My husband Gordon was a quiet chap like you. He
passed on two years ago. Morgan family used to own
this place. Their daughter had to go for a very rushed
holiday to Queensland — that's what they'd have you
believe, anyway. Must say your wife's a pretty little
thing, you been married long?

[BILL, *fed up with the harrassment, sticks his finger back in the flummery.*]

Might have to make another if you don't stop eating that one.

[BILL *chokes on the thought.*]

That's a bad cough. [*Eying his pyjamas*] You not well? Should keep well rugged up. I've got a couple of jumpers Gordon hardly wore, they might just fit you. I'll bring them over later. I've got tea on the stove so I won't stay and chat. Give my regards to your wife and if she needs to know anything about the district I'll fill her in. I'm only two houses up. It's the white one with the low fence. Wouldn't hang about in your bare feet if I were you. It won't do your cold any good. Nice talking to you.

[*She goes to leave.* BILL *picks up the bowl as if to hurl it at her and* FRANCES *enters carrying a large box.*]

Hallo, Molly Dwyer, two doors up.

FRANCES: Oh, Francine Clements.

MOLLY: Can I give you a hand?

[*She helps* FRANCES *with the box.*]

Hope you don't mind me barging in, but I've got tea on the stove. Dropped over a flummery.

[BILL *smiles and hands it to* FRANCES *who doesn't quite know what to do with it.*]

FRANCES: Oh, who ever would have thought . . . .

MOLLY: Your husband seems to like it.

FRANCES: Oh — he's not my husband.

MOLLY: Whatever, I'm not one to pass judgement. Each to his own. We were chatting about the neighbour-hood. If there's anything you want to know I've already told — erm . . .

BILL: Bill.

MOLLY: Bill, I'm only two doors up. You can see it from here.

[*They move over to the window.*]

The white one with the low fence. Directly next to you is the Demetrious family, don't speak much English, keep much to themselves except the little boy, George, don't take any lip from him. And on the other side's old Mr Archer. Well, better get back before my tea boils dry. Drop the bowl in any time you're passing. It's strawberry. This is a good district. Word of warning about the seagulls, though. Don't leave anything out on the line too long, they muck up the washing.

FRANCES: Bill is my brother. He's retarded.

BILL: It went right over her head.

MOLLY: Nice district, but watch the gulls. Bye, Billy.

> [FRANCES *watched* MOLLY *go. She laughs to herself, looks about the place and finally at* BILL.]

FRANCES: We'll be fine here, sport, just fine.

BILL: She'd come here with nothing much but a hope of something better, for both of us. I didn't know Frances, but I watched her those first few days, and she watched me.

> [FRANCES *re-enters with a box from the car.*]

She would smile, and I'd smile back a lot.

> [FRANCES *exits and the lights begin to change as the sound of the gulls is heard faintly in the distance.*]

I didn't dare move from this place — too scared — but I could see them out there. Their cries woke me first thing. At night I watched them through the window making shapes against the sea. One night Frances was next door . . . . I could hear them calling from the cliff tops . . . They beckoned me to step outside, join them.

> [*The harmonica plays and he looks skyward. He steps down onto the beach which fills with a bright white light as the two gulls appear at the back of the stage. He turns to watch as they fly toward the forestage. He walks up to meet them as the two gulls cross, circle him, and accompany him back down. He reaches out to touch one as it lands. The bird flies a few paces away and settles. He takes two steps towards it and the gull flies over his head and joins its companion as they perform a short aerial ballet.* BILL *laughs, takes a run at them; they cross in front of him,*

swoop to the other side, then out over the audience.
BILL *sits and watches them perform in the*
windstream as they parade up and down before him.
The lights at the rear of the stage fade completely as
two torch lights appear at the back of the house. The
gulls fly back toward the beach as the voices of
FRANCES *and* MOLLY *are heard calling for* BILL. *A*
torch shines on him.

MOLLY: Here he is, Frances. I've found him. Bloody gulls,
nick off!

[*They fly off either side.*]

FRANCES: Where are you?

MOLLY: Down the cliffs. Follow the path through.
[*Going over to* BILL] Where've you been, young man?
Running off like that. Your sister's been half mad with
worry.

[FRANCES *runs on.*]

FRANCES: Bill. Where have you been? Don't ever run off
like that again, Bill, you hear me? What are you doing
down here?

MOLLY: You been making sandcastles?

FRANCES: God you're freezing. Come on back to the
house, you'll catch your death down here. What on
earth were you doing?

[*As they move back toward the house the harmonica*
is heard in the distance. BILL *turns back to look for*
the gulls.]

What's the matter?

[*He points his finger in the air.*]

Birds, seagulls. You've seen seagulls before. Come on.

[*He doesn't move. The music comes to a sudden*
crescendo as the gulls fly across the back of the stage
in a flood of light. BILL *points to them.*]

MOLLY: Yes, birdies. You see them, you shoo them away.

FRANCES: Thank you for your help, Mrs Dwyer.

MOLLY: 'Molly', please.

FRANCES: Thank you.

[*They move back to the house.*]

MOLLY: We're going to see quite a bit of one another from

now on, Billy. Frances has asked me to keep an eye on you while she's working. How about that, eh?

BILL: Instantly, panic gripped me. I was sorely tempted to commit some outrageous act, squash the whole idea before it began. But I thought of Frances, gritted my teeth and . . .

[*He turns to them and smiles.*]

MOLLY: What's he saying?

FRANCES: He's saying thank you. Are you sure you won't take any money?

MOLLY: Don't embarrass me, Frances. [*To* BILL] We're going to become great chums, aren't we?

[BILL *smiles.*]

And don't give your sister another scare like tonight, young Billy.

BILL: Bill.

MOLLY: Yes. I'll have some nice lunch for you, too. Night, night, Billy.

BILL: It was always Bill before. Never Billy. Never.

[MOLLY *exits and the others enter the house.*]

FRANCES: Night, Molly. Get into bed, sport.

[*She watches him for a moment.*]

What were you doing down there?

[*She exits. The harmonica tingles as the gulls appear.*]

BILL: Of course, I'd seen gulls before. Every summer. But that was back then. Now, to see these creatures fly. They were like some magical god descending from the heavens. They could move over water. And I hadn't seen such creatures before. I hadn't witnessed this miracle. This freedom.

[*He looks briefly about the place.*]

Frances was right.

[*The birds fly off: the lights return to normal as* BILL *sits at the table.*]

It was the beginning for us.

[*The lights rise for morning as* FRANCES *enters from her bedroom area (off) with a pad, pencil and an old library book.*]

FRANCES: Come on, sport. [*Taking his hand*] You got the bread for the gulls?

[BILL *runs to the kitchen.*]

Don't run, just walk. We've got to learn how to walk first.

[*He re-emerges with a brown paper bag containing some stale bread. She takes his hand and they walk down to the beach.*]

We'll have to make do with the old library book again.

[*They settle down. She leafs through the book.*]

BILL: During those first weeks, the lessons on the beach became a daily ritual.

FRANCES: Reckon Mum and Dad taught you sweet bugger all.

BILL: Very much the blind leading the blind.

FRANCES: We'll stick with your name again. Repeat it after me sport, Bill. B-I-L-L.

[*He just stares at her.*]

Strewth, you haven't the foggiest what I'm talking about, have you? Bill, repeat it, Bill.

[*He smiles at her. She refers to the book.*]

I wish that book would arrive from England. Look, I'll write it in the sand. [*Doing so*] B-I-L-L. See, that's you. Christ, you know that's you, don't you? But say it. [*Pointing to the figures in the sand*] B-I-L-L. Say 'Bill'.

[*The sound of the harmonica, momentarily in the background, as the gulls are flying over.* BILL *looks up.*]

Come on, sport. Concentrate, Billy. Come on, B. Say 'B'.

[*He tries to say a 'B' sound*]

Good, great. Billy, see. [*Pointing to the name in the sand*] That's your name. See.

[*He bends over it, examining the word. A gull flies over. He looks up and stands.*]

No, Billy, concentrate. Sit down.

[*She takes hold of his hand and tries to pull him down. He resists.*]

Billy, sit down, it's only a seagull. Say 'B' again. B.

[*He messes up the name with his foot.* FRANCES *snaps at him angrily.*]

What did you do that for?

[*She calms herself down. She refers to the book then tosses it away.*]

This must have come out with the ark. Come on, sit down, we'll write it out again. Together.

[*She takes his hand and they both write out his name.*]

There's B; you can say 'B' . . . .

[*He attempts to.*]

Good. The next letter is 'I'.

[*They begin to write it out as the gulls fly out from either side of the forestage. He stands and watches them.*]

Sit down and concentrate, we'll feed the gulls after.

[*She takes his hand and he knocks it away.*]

Billy, sit down. Come on say 'I'. B-I . . .

BILL: Gill.

FRANCES: What did you say? Come on, say it again.

BILL: [*with great difficulty*] Gill.

[*The birds settle. He moves towards one.*]

FRANCES: Don't get too close, you'll scare it. Do you want to feed the gulls?

[*She takes the brown paper bag and offers it to him. He reaches out his hand to take it and she withdraws it.*]

Say the word again. Say it again first. Gulls.

BILL: [*holding out his hand*] Gill.

FRANCES: Gulls. [*Trying to contain her excitement and not frighten him or the birds*] Here you are. Give the bread to the gills.

[*He takes it.*]

No, no, gulls.

[*He stops.*]

Go on. Don't move too quickly.

BILL: Gulls.

[*He throws the bread toward them and they fly up and off. The harmonica fades.*]

FRANCES: They'll be back, sport. [*Hugging him*] The gulls will be back, they've just gone home. They'll be back. You will too, sport, you will too.

[DAN *calls from off stage.*]

DAN: Frances . . . [*Walking through the front door*] Frances, you in?

FRANCES: Oh my God.

DAN: You in there, Bill?

FRANCES: [*calling to him*] We're down the beach, Dan. [*She rushes to her bag and searches through it.*] It's Dan, Billy. Dan's come to visit.

DAN: [*walking through the house*] Whereabouts?

FRANCES: You can never find —

DAN: Hello.

[*He walks down to meet them.*]

FRANCES: Hello. What are you doing here?

DAN: Well, that's a warm welcome.

FRANCES: I mean, how did you find the place?

DAN: Some old lady up the road knew all about you.

FRANCES: Ha ha ha. Dan's met Mrs Dwyer, Billy.

DAN: No, she met me. G'day Bill. How you going, kid? [*He holds out his hand to him but* BILL *just stares at him.*] What's the matter?

FRANCES: He doesn't recognise you in these surroundings, that's all. Why didn't you let me know you were coming?

DAN: I didn't know myself.

FRANCES: Baloney.

DAN: Yes.

[*Pause.*]

FRANCES: Well?

DAN: What?

FRANCES: What do you think of the place?

DAN: . . . Good.

FRANCES: It's just the bare essentials, but give us time and we'll have it looking really smart, won't we, sport?

DAN: It looks fine.

FRANCES: It's a start.

[*Pause.*]

BILL: Reckon that's it for the lessons today.

DAN: What did he say?

FRANCES: We learnt a word today.

[*She moves over to* DAN *and holds him.*]

We actually learnt a word. Gulls. Already he's improving. It is for the better, Dan.

DAN: Maybe.

FRANCES: I'm glad you came down.

[*She kisses him.*]

Come in and I'll get you a beer.

DAN: Don't let me interrupt.

FRANCES: Oh, we've got plenty of time. I don't start in the library till next week. Come on, sport. That's it for today. We'll feed the gulls again tomorrow.

DAN: Oh, seagulls.

[DAN *points to the sky.* BILL *shakes his head, no.*]

What's that mean?

FRANCES: Dunno.

[BILL *walks over to* DAN *and blows a raspberry in his face, and then points in the direction the gulls flew off.*]

BILL: Gulls.

DAN: Oh, right, they flew off that way. Pretty dumb of me. Suppose you reckon I need to take a few lessons too?

[BILL *shrugs his shoulders,* DAN *laughs,* BILL *joins in, puts his arm around* DAN *and they walk off to the house.* FRANCES *collects the book and bag, looks down at the sand where the word is written and rubs it out with her feet.*]

FRANCES: We'll get back to that tomorrow.

[*She moves back to the house.* DAN *has entered, but* BILL *remains outside.*]

DAN: Where's that beer you promised me?

[*He goes and helps himself.*]

FRANCES: You want a beer, Billy?

[*He doesn't indicate either yes or no but continues to stare out to sea.* FRANCES *enters the house*]

Only a small one for me. House will come up pretty

well, won't it? I've got to get some re-wiring done, but it
rained two nights ago and all the guttering and down-
pipes are fine.

DAN: Here's to you. You're looking good, Frances.

FRANCES: And yesterday I pulled back that plasterboard
in the kitchen and the original pine linings are there.

DAN: I didn't come to talk about the house.

BILL: The door was shut on me.
  [*The lights change.*]
  It was his first trip to see us, and I had the door shut on
  me. Pretty bloody rude, I thought. I sat out here. They
  obviously didn't want me inside. I mean, you can't get
  more obvious than the back door being slammed in
  your face, can you? And I was really thirsty, I remember
  that. So I got up to go inside and . . . .
  [*The lights change.*]

FRANCES: I respected your decision; have the decency to
respect mine. I told you my answer before, and that
answer's still the same.

DAN: And I still don't accept it, or believe it.

FRANCES: Then you're the bloody fool, not him.
  [*The lights change.*]

BILL: So I sat down again. They did a hell of a lot of
screaming and yelling that afternoon, for two people
who supposedly liked one another. Then it all went
quiet. I stuck my head inside just as Dan went storming
out the front door.

DAN: Bye, Billy . . .

BILL: He jumped into his Holden, revved the shit out of
her, and tore off up the road. Frances didn't do
anything! She just stood there.
  [*He moves toward her. She moves away.*]

FRANCES: I . . . I need to go for a bit of a walk, Billy. Don't
leave the house. I'll be back . . .
  [*But she can't finish the sentence.* BILL *goes over to
  her and puts his arm around her shoulder.*]
  I won't be long . . .
  [*She wanders off to the beach.* BILL *sits at the table.*]

DAN: Frances didn't come back for an hour or two. Dan

got married pretty soon after to a lady called Elizabeth. I'd never met Elizabeth and we didn't go to the wedding but we gave her a present anyway. Frances said it was the thing to do. Frances was pretty funny that day too. It was about this time that Mrs Dwyer began figuring in my life in a big way.

MOLLY: [*offstage*] Cooee, Billy.

BILL: I'll sneak out the back way and try and avoid her.
[MOLLY *enters from the front as* BILL *disappears out the back and onto the beach.*]

MOLLY: Billy, where are you?
[*She looks through the house.*]

BILL: Perhaps if I just sit here quietly she'll go away.

MOLLY: Where the bloody hell's that kid?
[*She comes out the back.* BILL *disappears up the side.*]
You on the beach, Bill Clements? I've got your lunch.

BILL: [*racing across the front yard and out of sight*] No prizes for guessing what it'll be.
[*She goes back to the front door and sees him disappearing over the road.*]

MOLLY: Get on back here, Bill Clements. I haven't got all day. And watch when you cross the road.
[*She goes back inside.* BILL *comes racing onto the forestage and halts.*]

BILL: Didn't have to tell me that. Frances has drummed that into me. I'm proud of the fact that I can cross the road.
[BILL *enters the house as* MOLLY *prepares lunch.*]

MOLLY: Got your favourite today, Billy. 'A little Pecks goes such a long way'.

BILL: On the first day she looked after me, I stupidly ate all the sandwiches. Frances said I had to. It included a couple with fish paste. I left them, and she took this to mean I was saving my favourite till last. They featured heavily on the menu from that day on.
[*She places the sandwich before him then goes and turns on the television.*]

MOLLY: Just about time for *Doctor McIntyre*. Frances should get an electrician to look at this TV, their faces keep turning green.

BILL: *Doctor McIntyre* is Mrs Dwyer's favourite serial. We watch every episode while I dispose of the sandwiches.

MOLLY: Don't play with your food. Now what will Frances want in hers?

BILL: [*forcing one down*] I can tell you what she won't want.

MOLLY: You been feeding them seagulls. See if you can tell them to leave my washing alone. They've got all the beach to fly about in. That's a boy, eat them all up. This arthritis of mine isn't getting any better. Dr McIntyre, you can hang up your shingle here anytime. Do you remember what happened yesterday?

BILL: Dr McIntyre has a daughter called Grace, she doesn't know who to get engaged to: young Fred Watson — he's the local mechanic — or Bill Stevens — he's the local vet. Now — you don't want to hear all this, do you?

MOLLY: I wish Dr Andrews would watch this, he might pick up a few hints if he did.

BILL: Dr McIntyre had hands of magic, apparently.

MOLLY: He's got hands of magic, Billy. He'd be able to cure the arthritis.

[*Through this* BILL *has been secreting sandwiches in his pocket.*]

Grace won't listen to her father. She'll come to no good — have to take a 'holiday in Queensland' like the Morgan lass.

[BILL *has begun to play with himself, one hand on the table, the other in his dressing-gown pocket. He is staring at* MOLLY's *breasts.*]

You made quick work of that, young man, want any more? Want any more of your Aunty Molly's sandwiches? [*Pointing to her mouth and pretending to eat*] More?

[BILL *tries to say no.*]

Strewth, does that mean yes or no? [*Repeating the gesture*] More?

[BILL *tries to say no again.* MOLLY *shakes her head in a yes and no fashion.*]

Yes or no?

[BILL *repeats both gestures and emits a garbled reply.*]

No, Billy, not both. This means yes and this means no. You know that. I've seen you talk to Frances like that, so what is it? [*Repeating both gestures*] Yes or no?

BILL: What I'm trying to tell her is, 'Yes I'd like some more but not fish paste'.

[*As he is saying the quote, he nods his head up and down then side to side, then takes one of the sandwiches out of his pocket and puts it back on the plate.*]

MOLLY: Where did that come from? Stand up, young man.

[*He remains seated. She takes him by the ear and pulls him off the chair.*]

Billy, stand up. Now you, empty those pockets. Billy, empty those pockets.

[*He just stands there staring at her breasts still with one hand in his pocket.*]

Very well, young man. [*Diving her hand into his pocket.*]

Oh my God. Oooh. [*Pulling out several sandwiches stuck together*] What are these?

[*He sits.*]

Stand up! What do you mean by this? You been saving these for them bloody gulls, haven't you?

[*He tries to move away again. She grabs him.*]

I haven't finished with you yet.

[*She thrusts her hand into his other pocket.* BILL *smiles and puts his hand on her breast. She screams and jumps back several paces clutching more mangled sandwiches.*]

You dirty little bugger. That's what you are. A dirty little boy.

[*He puts his hand back in his pocket and continues to masturbate.*]

Take — your hand out — of your pyjamas, you dirty old man.

BILL: What a triumph. Someone had actually admitted I was old. A fully grown man.

MOLLY: Did you hear me? Take your hand out — oh, I can't look.

[*She goes and turns the television off.*]

How long have you been throwing away good food to those birds? [*Hurling a sandwich at him*] Are you listening to me?

[*He tries to speak.*]

Stop making those ridiculous noises, Billy.

[*He is nearing climax.*]

And take your hand out of your pyjamas. Wait till your sister gets home.

[*He stops masturbating.*]

You do understand me. [*Pointing her finger at him*] You understand all right when you want to.

BILL: I just want to feel your breast.

MOLLY: Stop making those silly noises. What are you staring at?

[BILLY *puts his hand in the other pocket.*]

I warn you, Billy, I warn you. You do understand me, I know.

[*He takes a small, dead seagull out of his pocket and offers it to her. It is a tiny chick.*]

What's — oh my God, you've been robbing nests.

[*He moves toward her holding the dead gull out in the flat of his hand.* MOLLY *backs away until she is flat to the wall.*]

Take that thing outside this instant. Do you hear me, Billy, take that dead bird outside.

[*He smiles and tries to say, 'gull'.*]

We'll forget this all happened if you take the dead birdy back down . . .

[*He holds the dead bird up to her face. She screams and lashes out at him. With his other hand he lifts her dress and thrusts his hand upward.* FRANCES *races in carrying some books.*]

FRANCES: Oh, Christ — Billy!

[*She pulls him away from* MOLLY *who is quite hysterical.*]

Billy . . .

[*She pushes him aside and tries to comfort* MOLLY.]

Molly, are you all right?

[*She shies away from* FRANCES.]

MOLLY: That filthy cretin had his hand up my dress.

[FRANCES *tries again to comfort her and* MOLLY *again pushes her away.*]

FRANCES: Molly, please sit. . .

MOLLY: That dirty bastard tried to rape me.

[FRANCES *moves to* BILL.]

FRANCES: Billy, get into your bedroom.

[MOLLY *moves over and stops him from going into his room.*]

MOLLY: No.

[*He turns away from* MOLLY. *She grabs hold of his sleeve.*]

Look at me.

[*She pulls him around to face her.*]

Look at me in the eye.

[*She slaps him across the face.*]

Discipline. We need to learn more discipline.

[*She moves over to the table and collects her things.*]

FRANCES: I'm so sorry —

[MOLLY *puts her hand up to silence her.*]

MOLLY: Will I see you tomorrow lunchtime?

[*She looks over to* BILL. *He merely looks up to her.*]

Good. We'll forget this ever happened.

[*She goes.*]

BILL: Forget? Oh no, please. Don't pretend it didn't happen, please.

[*He clutches himself as if in pain.*]

MOLLY: Afternoon, Frances.

FRANCES: Billy, come and sit down. Come on, I'm not going to hit you. I just want to talk to you.

[*He sits at the table.*]

Nod your head up and down if you understand me,

sport.

[*He does so and she takes his hand.*]

You mustn't do that ever again. You understand me?
Never. Mrs Dwyer's our friend. She's the only one to
look after you while I'm at work. You can't — force —
onto, erm . . . People must be attracted — oh, God. Mrs
Dwyer's already married.

[BILL *tries to speak.* FRANCES *puts her hand to his
mouth.*]

Don't make those noises, Billy, you know I don't
understand what you're trying to say. Don't get excited,
I can't make out what you're trying to tell me.

[*He again tries to speak.* FRANCES *snaps at him.*]

Billy, just shut up.

[BILL *continues to babble.* FRANCES *bangs the
table and yells at him.*]

Billy, shut up.

[*They pause for a second.*]

For God's sake, you get urges, I understand that,
but Mrs Dwyer's an elderly woman. Christ, how do I
explain this? Do you remember Mum and Dad, Billy?
Dad died, didn't he?

[BILL *nods yes.*]

Well, Mrs Dwyer's husband is dead like Dad, and soon
Mrs Dwyer will be dead too.

[BILL *nods his head up and down and smiles.*]

Billy, it's not funny. I'm trying to . . . We don't want
Mrs Dwyer to die.

[BILL *cocks his head to one side and looks at her.*]

OK, who would look after you when I'm at the library?
It would be back to the hostel, sport. Think that one
over. [*Taking his hand*] Give me your hand. [*Placing it
on her breast*] That's nice, isn't it?

[*He nods yes.*]

But I'm your sister, Billy, We can't do that, like you
can't do that with Mrs Dwyer.

[*He begins to protest.*]

I know he's dead; but, sport — there is no way it can
happen. You are too big for me to control when you try

to break out. I don't want to send you back to the hostel, but if you don't try . . .

[*He starts to make a noise and rock back and forth in his seat.*]

Stop that, stop making those noises.

[*He becomes louder.*]

Billy, I'm not saying you'll have to go back.

[*He starts to bang his head up and down on the table.*]

Billy, don't do that.

[*She gets up and tries to hold him. He fights against her. The harmonica plays and the gulls appear in the background.*]

I'm not going to send you away, Billy.

[*He tosses her off and races out the door and down to the beach.* FRANCES *stops at the verandah and calls after him.*]

Billy! Come back, Billy!

[*The gulls fly down onto the forestage.* BILL *falls to his knees with a cry of anguish. The gulls circle above his head. He tries to write something in the sand, tries to say the word. He clutches his knees and huddles in the sand as the gulls swoop desperately above him and the lights slowly fade.*]

END OF ACT ONE

ACT TWO

Dusk. BILL *is sitting on the beach, back to the audience. The sound of the waves can be heard breaking in the background. The music gently merges with the sound of the waves as the gulls rise in the background circling one another, swoop to the front and fly off.* BILL *stands, spins about and strikes a debonair pose. He is wearing a jacket and trousers.*

BILL: What do you reckon? Pretty nifty, eh?
    [*He walks down to the forestage and chats to the audience.*]
   This isn't new, though. Frances got me the pants for Mum's funeral and the blazer used to belong to Mrs Dwyer's Gordon. [*Looking at the insignia on the pocket*] It was his old bowls jacket, I think. Gordon was quite a bit smaller than me.
    [*He parades up and down, obviously proud of his almost new garments.*]
   Still, it's not too bad. Not too bad at all. Dressed like this, Frances reckons I look more handsome than Victor Mature — she always had a bit of a passion for him — but I think it's more David Niven, what do you reckon?
    [FRANCES *enters from her bedroom, partially dressed.*]
FRANCES: Billy . . .
BILL: We'd been shopping.
FRANCES: God, where is that kid?
BILL: She knows I'll be down here.
FRANCES: You down the beach?
BILL: See.
FRANCES: Come back inside.
BILL: I'll pretend not to hear.
    [*He goes to cover his ears.*]
FRANCES: And don't pretend you can't hear.
BILL: No flies on Frances.

[*He looks toward the house to see if* FRANCES *is looking out for him. Seeing she isn't he turns back to the audience.*]

We went shopping in town. Dan took us.

[DAN *enters from the bedroom.*]

He started visiting again. He's a father now; had a little girl. Wouldn't call her Bill, named her Joanna instead. Mind you, he didn't buy me much. Frances, on the other hand, got quite a few presents. Oh, she bought me some new underpants, and a pad with Jane Russell on the front. I like Jane Russell's tits. And I got lost. That was fun. Frances got pretty upset, though. I didn't think I was lost. I was just fascinated by the dairy snow ice cream dispenser. It's magical. Never seems to run out. Mine melted all over my hand.

FRANCES: Will you see what's holding Billy up?

DAN: [*calling out the back*] Hey, Billy, get up here. I've got to go soon.

[FRANCES *walks over to him and finishes doing up his shirt buttons.*]

BILL: Hoo-bloody-ray. He wasn't actually coming to see *me* any more. They weren't fooling anybody; they thought they were, though. You know when you get a feeling about something? Well I got this feeling.

DAN: Come on, sport.

[FRANCES *begins to prepare the evening meal.*]

BILL: He's also taken to calling me 'sport'. Frances calls me sport, I like that. She's always called me 'sport'. It's her word for me, not his.

DAN: Your present's waiting to be opened.

BILL: Six pairs of Y-front BVD's. Can hardly contain the excitement.

[DAN *looks at his watch.*]

DAN: Is there a garage open late? I'm almost out of petrol.

FRANCES: You could always stay the night.

DAN: I think there's one in Geelong. Yes, I think there is.

[FRANCES, *who is peeling the potatoes, comes to a momentary halt, doesn't look up, then continues on.*]

FRANCES: Knock on the Williams' door, they'll open up for you. How many potatoes?

DAN: What?

FRANCES: How many potatoes do you want?

DAN: None for me.

FRANCES: You sure?

DAN: We're on a diet.

FRANCES: Oh, are we?

DAN: Yes, well, just watching our . . .

FRANCES: I didn't know. Not even one?

DAN: No, I can't have any.

FRANCES: Surely one won't do any harm?

DAN: You know I can't stay the night.

BILL: I'm sure she never meant to get this involved.

FRANCES: I wouldn't have bought so many if — I mean I would have got you . . .

DAN: Frances, please. This has to be my last trip.

[*She stops what she is doing.* BILL *walks to the back door and bangs his feet on the ground.*]

FRANCES: That you, Billy?

BILL: I'm knocking the sand off my feet, sorta like ringing the door bell.

[*He enters.*]

FRANCES: About time. I want no more trouble from you today. You almost gave me a heart attack when you got lost.

BILL: [*directly to* FRANCES] I wasn't lost, I was watching an ice cream machine till the girl told me to bugger off.

FRANCES: Enough of that. It's time for your practice. Come on, fifteen minutes.

[FRANCES *moves in and out getting* BILL'*s book and pad. He follows her, berating her as she goes.*]

BILL: Had to stand in the lingerie department while you went through every bloody bra and girdle in the shop. God, was that ever embarrassing but did I complain?

FRANCES: Enough. Open your pad and practise. Your name. Write your name. Where's your pencil?

DAN: I've got one here.

FRANCES: Open your pad and show Dan. Go on. Show Dan.

BILL: Oh God no, here we go. Freak show time.

DAN: [*giving* BILL *a pencil*] Here's a pencil.

BILL: [*holding it up to the audience*] No, really, this a pencil?

[*He goes to open the pad but is caught by the cover.*] Jane Russell, you have got the best tits.

FRANCES: Your book came in the mail. We'll start on that tomorrow.

DAN: Frances . . .

FRANCES: I've got to get dinner cooking if you're leaving soon.

DAN: Have you understood a word I've said to you?

BILL: Things were changing in our house.

MOLLY: [*off*] Cooee.

DAN: Christ, get rid of her.

MOLLY: You in, Frances?

FRANCES: Come through, Molly.

MOLLY: Evening all, have a nice trip to town? Something smells good.

FRANCES: Have you eaten, Molly?

MOLLY: Thank you very much, Frances, I'd love to.
[*She sits.*]

BILL: [*without looking up, still writing*] Well, that solved the problem of the potatoes.

DAN: How are you keeping, Molly?

MOLLY: Not well, Dan, not well.

BILL: [*looking up and directing this straight at the audience*] This could take some time, so feel free to stretch your legs, clear your throat, have a scratch, whatever.

MOLLY: And now I've got a new set of tablets to keep the blood pressure down. What are you gurgling about, young man?

DAN: He's trying to write his name.

MOLLY: [*picking up the pad*] You write that? Better than yesterday's effort.

DAN: Great, sport, you'll be prime minister yet.

MOLLY: Let's not get carried away. Wait till he can put the B's around the right way. Want me to set the table?

FRANCES: Thanks.

[MOLLY *does so and begins to put the place mats out.* BILL *watches her out of the corner of his eye.*]

MOLLY: I've got a bone to pick with you, Bill Clements. Those mates of yours were hanging about this afternoon waiting to be fed. Spotted every sheet I washed.

BILL: I've been training them for months.

MOLLY: You laughing at me? Sometimes I reckon you're in league with those birds, don't you Dan?

DAN: Yes.

MOLLY: And how's your wife? Elizabeth well?

DAN: Fine, she's fine.

MOLLY: And little Joanna, how's my darling?

DAN: Good, she's good.

MOLLY: Must be nearly six months now.

DAN: Mmmmm.

MOLLY: Got a photo yet? You promised me a photo.

DAN: [*reaching into his wallet*] Right.

MOLLY: Oh, isn't she lovely? Isn't she lovely, Frances?

FRANCES: [*continuing to prepare the meal*] Yes.

MOLLY: She's got her father's eyes, hasn't she?

DAN: Yes.

MOLLY: When are you bringing her down to meet her Aunty Molly?

DAN: Soon. One day soon.

MOLLY: You should bring them both down for a visit one day.

[FRANCES *goes and gets the book.*]

DAN: I will.

MOLLY: They must miss you being away so much. You going back tonight?

FRANCES: [*re-entering and plonking the book down beside* MOLLY] The book arrived, Molly. I'll set out a lesson and you can start tomorrow.

[MOLLY *just leans on the book.*]

MOLLY: Such a pretty thing.

FRANCES: Have a look.

[*She takes the photo,* MOLLY *opens the book.*]
Billy, finish setting the table.

[*She hands the photo back to* DAN. BILL *gets up and surveys the table.*]

MOLLY: Gawd strewth, look at the photos of these people. You sure you got the right book sent out? He doesn't look like this.

DAN: Brain's the same.

[BILL *removes one of the place mats from the table.*]

MOLLY: I wouldn't want to meet any of these boys on a dark night. D'you remember the kid over the other side to town? You know, past the gas works?

FRANCES: They were pulled down before we shifted here.

MOLLY: Oh.

DAN: [*to* FRANCES] Want a sherry?

MOLLY: No, thanks.

[FRANCES *nods her head, yes.*]

He looked just like this lad here. Frightful bloody business. Used to see them down the shops, he'd be tagging along behind her. She wasn't much brighter. Never saw that woman when she wasn't either pregnant or carrying one in her arms. No no, they belong in a home, eh, Dan?

FRANCES: Don't just stand there, Billy. Finish setting the table!

MOLLY: She needs to get out a bit more, doesn't she, Dan? You might meet someone that way. Some nice bloke, eh, Dan?

DAN: Yes.

MOLLY: You look tired, doesn't she? She's not an un-attractive woman, is she?

DAN: Pardon?

MOLLY: [*talking as if* FRANCES *were not in the room*] Frances, she's not an unattractive woman.

DAN: Definitely not.

MOLLY: [*looking back at the photos*] It'd scare any reasonable man off.

FRANCES: Go change out of your good clothes, sport.

MOLLY: Let me have a look at you before you go. Not

every day we see you dressed up to the nines.

[BILL *stops and turns toward her.*]

Oh yes, very nice.

FRANCES: More handsome than Victor Mature.

MOLLY: Victor Mature never wore a suit. He was always in those funny little dresses, you know, like in Quo Thingo.

[BILL *turns to go.*]

FRANCES: What have you got in your pockets?

[*He continues walking until she addresses him.*]

Billy.

DAN: I bought him a bag of crumble bar.

FRANCES: There'll be chocolate all over the inside of your pocket. Give them here.

[BILL *puts his hand over his pocket.*]

You got something in there you don't want me to see?

MOLLY: Strewth, not again.

[*He turns to go to his room.*]

DAN: Billy, give the chocolate to Frances.

[BILLY *looks at* FRANCES.]

FRANCES: Go on.

[*He empties his pocket. There is a comb, a dinky toy, a few sweets, and no crumble bars.*]

Did you buy them for him?

DAN: No.

MOLLY: He's been shoplifting.

FRANCES: Molly, let me handle this. Did you take those? Did you?

[*He nods yes.*]

Without paying for them?

[*He nods yes.*]

I've told you that's stealing. You know that, don't you? How many times . . ? Give them to me.

[*He hands the contraband over.*]

That everything?

[*He nods yes.*]

Right, no dinner tonight. Out of those clothes and into bed.

MOLLY: I know what I'd do if he were my kid.

FRANCES: Well, he's not, so just bloody well stay out of it.

MOLLY: [*to* DAN] Someone got out of the wrong side of bed this morning and it wasn't me.

DAN: Look, I might get going.

FRANCES: So soon?

DAN: I wasn't having any . . .

MOLLY: You not staying for tea?

FRANCES: Billy, go to your room.

DAN: There's a long drive back to —

FRANCES: It'd only take fifteen minutes. Go to your room.

MOLLY: You can't let him go without some food in his stomach.

FRANCES: Molly, please —

MOLLY: Come on, sit down.

> [*She pulls a chair out.*]

DAN: No.

FRANCES: I'll make you a sandwich. [*Moving off to do so*] Go to your room.

DAN: I don't want any.

MOLLY: He's only set three places, will you look at that?

FRANCES: [*to* MOLLY] Would you help Billy change?

DAN: No need, I'm going.

MOLLY: Don't go, I'll —

DAN: Will you both shut up!

> [*Silence.*]

I have dinner waiting for me at home. Goodbye, Molly.

MOLLY: Drive carefully. See you next time.

FRANCES: [*as* DAN *is going*] I'll see you to the—

DAN: No. Please, no.

> [*He goes.* FRANCES *goes a few paces then stops.*]

MOLLY: [*calling after him*] My love to Elizabeth and Joanna.

> [FRANCES *remains in the doorway.* MOLLY *walks into* BILL's *room. He is sitting on the side of the bed still clothed.*]

Look what you done now. Acting like a spoilt kid.

> [FRANCES *storms back inside.*]

FRANCES: Stop calling him a kid and stay out of what's not your concern. He's a fully grown man. See.

MOLLY: Got the brain of a kid, though, and that's something you're never going to change.

[FRANCES *moves away;* MOLLY *pursues her.*]

Not all the books in the world.

[FRANCES *gets the roast out of the oven and plonks it on the table.*]

FRANCES: I hope you like lamb because there's plenty of it.

MOLLY: You'll never find a man that'll take second place to that.

FRANCES: What?

MOLLY: I didn't come down in the last shower, young lady.

FRANCES: This is none of your business.

MOLLY: I'm making it mine. I look after him enough.

FRANCES: And for that I'm grateful.

MOLLY: Never seen one of them so-called friends down the library so much as lift a finger to help.

FRANCES: I wouldn't ask them.

MOLLY: But you would me.

FRANCES: That's not it at all.

MOLLY: What is it, then? It's all right for me to come in every other day.

FRANCES: I offered to pay for your time.

MOLLY: I don't want your money.

FRANCES: And I don't want to discuss it.

[FRANCES *hurls some potatoes into a saucepan or onto a serving plate.* MOLLY *pauses before casually dropping the next piece of ammunition.*]

MOLLY: He wanted to marry you once, didn't he?

FRANCES: You think it is as simple as that? You don't know the first thing, you just don't know.

MOLLY: I know you're making your life a bloody misery and it needn't be.

FRANCES: [*walking away*] I don't want to continue—

MOLLY: Hide from it. That's right, stick your head in the sand.

FRANCES: My personal life has nothing to do with you.

MOLLY: He still loves you, doesn't he? Any fool can see it. And you threw it all away because of that.

FRANCES: Don't you think I've been through all this a thousand times before? 'What if this, what if that? Maybe this, perhaps that', all night till it's impossible to sleep. Don't you think I have, you stupid woman? No, I accept that responsibility; and if you think that was an easy decision to make you're even stupider than I thought. Billy is like he is and I accept that fact; I'm thankful I still have him, no matter what state. But I wish other people would too and stop shoving their tuppenny-halfpenny advice down my throat and leave me alone.

MOLLY: You get no thanks for being a martyr, Frances, and that's what you're turning into.

FRANCES: [*slapping her across the face*] Get out.
[*Silence.*]

MOLLY: I'm not taking any more from you, young lady. [*Storming toward the door*] You know he'd be better off dead than left in that state.
[*She exits. She re-enters.*]
I'm stupid, am I? You can't get your own life into order and yet you think you can run someone else's. You're buggering up both of them. He'll have to go one day, you know that, don't you? Come pretty close a couple of times, already. He won't be beaten up or thrown in a dungeon. Wouldn't know the difference if he was. He's ignorant. You're both bloody ignorant. So what if he's your brother, what good's a boy like that to anyone? And don't point your finger at me and say I'm a hard old biddy. I'm being practical. I love him too, you know. I don't mind looking after him. I've had my life. But what will you have to show for it all, eh? Do you think he's suddenly going to turn around and thank you when you're a woman my age with nothing to show but a lot of wasted years? Do you reckon he is? If he could speak he'd curse you!
[*In the other room* BILL *emits an anguished wail as he throws himself to the floor.*]

FRANCES: Christ Almighty. [*Rushing into him*] It's all right, Billy. It's all right. Don't pull against me, sport.

Hold onto me, that's right, hold onto me, sport.
[*Holding him in her arms*] Good, good. Have you been
listening to Molly?
      [*He tries to break away again.*]
Hey, come on.
      [*He stands up and moves away from her.*]
That's how ignorant he is, Molly.
      [*He has his back to them but indicates with his hand
      for them to go.*]
Do you want us to get out.
      [*He nods his head up and down.*]
MOLLY: Billy . . .
FRANCES: [*putting her hand up to stop her*] You're
coming on just fine, sport, just fine. Do you believe me?
      [*There is no reply.*]
MOLLY: You're coming on good, Billy. Real good. Yes.
      [*He indicates for them to please leave his room.*]
FRANCES: OK, we're going.
MOLLY: I'm sorry . . .
FRANCES: You be right to change, don't need a hand?
      [*He shakes his head, no.*]
Say good night to Molly.
      [*They get no reply.*]
MOLLY: Will I see you in the morning? We got that book
from England to start on.
      [*After a moment he nods his head.*]
FRANCES: Good. Get changed now, sport.
MOLLY: Good night.
      [MOLLY *goes to exit.* FRANCES *remains in what is*
      BILL'*s doorway. He still has his back to them.*]
FRANCES: Thank you for all the time you spend with him.
MOLLY: I care about you. I care about you both.
      [MOLLY *goes.*]
FRANCES: Want a sherry, sport?
      [FRANCES *looks out of* BILL'*s window.*]
Come here, Bill.
      [*No reaction.*]
Please.
      [*He goes over to her, doesn't look up.*]

I really don't know what I'd do without you.

[*He places one hand on her shoulder.*]

Doesn't the beach look beautiful? Hardly a cloud in the sky. And look, look at the stars in the water. My God. [*Looking up*] We're like the head of a pin compared to all that. Things we do and say don't mean much when you look out there and see how really small and insignificant we are compared to that universe. It truly is an amazing place.

[BILL *puts his finger to her face and outlines it.*]

Yeah, we're pretty amazing too, sport. Pretty amazing.

[BILL *goes to the bed and gets something from under the pillow; puts his hand behind his back, walks to* FRANCES *and puts his free hand over her eyes.*]

What are you doing? Oh right, they're closed.

[*He takes out a set of gaudy beads and holds them to his neck and tries to speak 'for you'.* FRANCES *opens her eyes.*]

Did you . . . ?

[*He smiles and places them around her neck.* FRANCES *laughs.*]

Dan's right, you'd make a very good prime minister.

[BILL *smiles and nods in agreement.*]

Into bed. You want a hand to change?

[*He has only taken off his shoes and jumper. He shakes his head, no.*]

Sweet dreams, sweet repose, half the bed and all the clothes. Nigh'-night.

[BILL *falls back onto his bed.*]

BILL: Oh no.

[*The lights go down on* BILL's *room as* FRANCES *takes the leg of lamb from the table.*]

FRANCES: Cold lamb for the next week.

[*It falls from her hands. She sits.* FRANCES *finally breaks down.*]

Billy . . .

[*The lights fade. Lights up in* BILL's *room, he sits up in bed.*]

BILL: If a man kills a chook because it's ill and diseased

that's called humane. But if you kill a man who's ill and diseased that's called murder. Why? Because we can think much better than an animal can — most of the time. We feel things, we have emotions. But you only kill that chook, or the horse that's broken its leg, because it's in pain and it's releasing it from that pain to kill it. I'm not in any pain, physical pain. Frances is about the only one around here who's in pain. She doesn't think she is, though. She's doing it because she loves me. Mrs Dwyer thinks she's doing it out of duty. She may be right in part. But Frances is no martyr. She doesn't walk around wearing sack cloth and ashes. Would it be right to kill me? Leave me in a home? Or for a doctor to have just let me go? Would that have been the best thing to do? Mrs Dwyer's right on that one. Frances would have been married by now, probably have a tribe of kids too. All she's got now is me. That's her decision. Wasn't mine. Those people in the book, the photos Mrs Dwyer was looking at, would it be right to let them go? Would that be murder too? Or would it be saving someone else a lot of pain? Stranger things are done in the name of love. Frances must have thought about this a lot. I haven't. If someone were to walk up to me and go to break my neck, I'd fight back. I'd know they'd be trying to kill me. And I want to live. But if someone came up to me in the middle of the night and stuck a needle in me so I wouldn't wake up again ever, [*turning to* FRANCES] I wouldn't know. I'd just sleep on. Forever. It's fear that stops so many things, like love. But fear and love are just emotions. I'm sure when a chook sees a fox it feels fear too.

> [*Lights up to full. Morning.* FRANCES *gets up from the chair and begins to clear up.*]

FRANCES: Come on, sport, don't dilly dally in there. I'm running late.

> [*She runs into his bedroom. He is putting on his shoes. She takes over the procedure.*]

Shoe.

BILL: Shoe.

FRANCES: What's next? Look at the chart, remember.

BILL: Jumper.

[*He reaches for it and puts it on.*]

FRANCES: Other shoe. Now, when Mrs Dwyer comes I don't want any carry-on. OK? You won't need that today.

[*She pulls off his jumper.*]

BILL: But it was on the right way?

FRANCES: That's right. Shirt, pants, shoe.

[BILL *nods and* FRANCES *goes into the other room.*]

I've set out your lesson on this paper. Understand? The book's on the table. Here's money for an ice cream, but only after lunch. I'll be home about three-thirty and we'll go through the lesson again, eh? It's hot out so don't forget your hat.

[BILL *nods.*]

MOLLY: Cooee.

[MOLLY *comes into view carrying a basket and wearing an old sun hat.*]

FRANCES: Now remember what I said.

[MOLLY *stands at the back door.*]

MOLLY: Morning, Frances.

FRANCES: Come through, Molly.

[MOLLY *enters the house.*]

The book's on the table, if you get stuck, I've marked the chapter.

[FRANCES *goes to her room, still talking, to get her bag, etc.*]

There's a Thermos of tea for you, he's got his money for an ice cream, but only after lunch. Anything you don't understand, skip over.

[*She dashes out the door.*]

I'll be back about three-thirty, and could you make sure he keeps his hat on, it's going to be a scorcher. 'Bye.

[*But she is already out of sight.*]

MOLLY: Right.

[BILL *wanders into the kitchen holding his hat in his hand.*]

Morning, Billy. [*Taking the hat and placing it on his head*] No good in your hand. You get the chair from round the back while I load up.

    [*He goes.*]

What's all this?

    [*She picks up the book and places it in her bag.*]

She left any stale bread out for your gulls?

BILL: They can have my sandwiches.

MOLLY: No. They can go without, then.

    [*She exits.*]

Needn't think we're going to have all our lessons on the beach, this is only special. Don't drag it, things like that cost money. I said a few things last night you shouldn't have heard but you did and I'm not sorry I said them. Didn't mean anything against you. I was saying them for the benefit of Frances. Lot of bloody good it did. Don't dawdle. [*Coming to a halt*] Where do you want to sit?

    [BILL *points to the left,* MOLLY *doesn't even look where he is pointing and heads straight to the right.*]

Over here looks a good spot.

BILL: She'd be quite happy talking to a brick wall, only brick walls can't nod.

MOLLY: Don't make those funny noises.

BILL: I left my pad at home.

    [*He tries to explain.*]

MOLLY: Don't argue, we're going to sit here.

    [*She takes the book out of her bag and settles down in the chair.*]

Now, what's all this devastating knowledge we've been waiting so long for?

BILL: Where are you, gulls?

MOLLY: 'Disinhibition and masturbatioooo — ooh, God Almighty? Who'd want to know about that? I thought your sister said this was an education book. She's waited months for a book on that.

BILL: Have to keep the old doodle on the slack today.

MOLLY: Get away, you wretched blowies.

    [*She hits at them with the book, and the paper*

marker flies out.]
Bloody hell, where's this go?

[*She searches through the book muttering to herself.*]
'The patient should be asked to name objects.' — that
doesn't sound right. 'Ask the patient to repeat sentence'
What's Frances on about? You can't speak. She's, she's
got the wrong book. Months of waiting and she's
ordered the wrong book. Can't she do nothing right?
[*Reading from the slip of paper*] 'If you have any time
over, demonstrate with some article a simple situation
of purchase.' [*Dropping the book*] She should ask for
her money back on that one. 'Explain the process
simply, until the basic principle is understood.' We
don't have to be a genius to work out what this is in aid
of, do we? This is more our level. You know about
buying things. We bought things down the shops
together.

[MOLLY *begins to organise the shop.*]
Right, I'll be Mr Williams down the shops and you
want to buy something. Got any money?

[BILL *smiles at her.*]
That mean you have or you haven't?

[*He shows it to her.*]
That your ice cream money?

[BILL *nods.*]
Right, what do you want to buy?

[BILL *surveys the goods and shakes his head in the
negative.*]
No, Billy, you've got to buy something, what do you
want?

[*He puts his money back in his pocket.*]
Want to buy this book? Personally I wouldn't give
you two bob for it. What about this chair, or the
Thermos?

[BILL *continually shakes his head, no.*]
This isn't a game, too bloody hot for games. Take that
smile off your face before I wipe it off. We'll start again.
I'm Mr Williams.

[BILL *laughs.*]

What's so bloody funny? Oh I see, ha, ha, all right, I'm
Mrs Williams. Good morning, Mr Clements, what can
I get for you?

BILL: I'd like an ice cream, please.

MOLLY: Don't make those sounds. Point to what you
want.

[BILL *points to the chair.*]

Oh, this Thermos? It's a very good Thermos, Mr
Clements, keeps things either hot or cold. How's your
sister Frances and that lovely Mrs Dwyer, she well?
That'll be twenty-five cents please.

[*She holds out the Thermos toward him with one
hand and keeps the other flat to receive the money.*]

Here, take it.

[*He does so.*]

You've got to give me the money. It's not free.

[*He thrusts the Thermos back into her hands.*]

I don't want it, I want the money. There you are, Mr
Clements, that'll be twenty-five cents, please. Give me
the money.

[BILL *shakes his head, no.*]

Repeat the process? We'll be here all bloody day.
Look, I'll be you and you be Mrs Williams. Get that
side of the counter and sell me the Thermos.

[*She takes money out of the bag and pushes him to
the other side of the counter.*]

Good morning, Mrs Williams. Isn't it a nice day? Bit
too hot for my liking, really. That's a nice frock you're
wearing. How's your arthritis? Mine played up badly
last night. Is that a Thermos you're holding? That's
just what I want. How much?

BILL: Five hundred and eighty seven billion dollars and
eleven cents.

MOLLY: Twenty-five cents? That sounds reasonable to
me. Here you are, don't bother to wrap it. I'll take it
as it is.

[*She takes the Thermos and gives* BILL *the money.*]

Give my regards to Mr Williams. Good morning.

[*She pretends to walk out of the shop.*]

See? Can't make it any simpler than that. Here, now
you buy it from me.

[BILL *shakes his head, no*]

What do you mean, no? It's your turn.

[BILL *puts the money in his pocket.*]

Take that money out of your pocket and give it back
to me.

[BILL *points to the Thermos.*]

Yes, I know I bought the Thermos but that was
pretends. Frances owns the Thermos. Why would I
want to buy it?

[BILL *shrugs his shoulders and sits.*]

I've got a Thermos. I don't need one. Here, you buy
it back and I'll keep your money, see how you feel about
that.

[*She puts the Thermos on the ground beside him. He
looks at it then pushes it away.*]

We are not moving from this beach till you give me
my money. [*Sitting in the chair*] We can sit
here all night for all I care. Go without your
tea. Just wait till Frances hears about this little
act you've bunged on. Won't be so cocky then.
[*Picking up the book*] The months she waited
for this codswollop. Not worth sixpence.

[*She tosses the book onto the ground.* BILL *retrieves
it.*]

What do you think you're doing?

[*He reaches in his pocket and tosses her a coin.*]

Five cents? Very funny. You're not as dumb as you
make out, young man. Give me my other twenty cents.

[BILL *shakes his head, no.*]

This is the last time I'll be taking you for any lessons,
Mr Bill Clements. No more lunch, no more —

[*The music plays and the gulls rise from the back
of the house.* BILL*'s face lights up as he looks out to
sea.*]

That's another thing, I catch you feeding those wretched birds near my place again I'll tan your hide.

[BILL *moves up toward them as they fly down past*

the house.]

Give me my money.

[*He looks up at them as* MOLLY *runs over and dives her hand in his pocket. He brushes her aside and moves to the basket and takes out the sandwiches.*]

Don't you push me. How dare you push me? You were warned what would happen last time.

[BILL *holds the sandwiches up in the air. The gulls circle around.*]

Put those sandwiches back in the basket, Bill Clements.

[MOLLY *tries to shoo them away.*]

Get away from here. Go on, buzz off. Leave my lunch alone, you birds. Get out of it.

[*The birds fly off and* BILL *looks in amazement at* MOLLY.]

That is not for them birds. That is our lunch. Put them back in the bag, give me my money and get up to the house.

[BILL *drops the sandwiches on the ground and slams his foot on them.*]

You've just pushed your luck too far.

[*She packs up her bag and chair.*]

You know darn well what you're doing and you're doing everything in your power to be a contrary little bugger. Well, no more. I've had it up to here.

[MOLLY *is stomping off when she comes to a halt.*]

Bugger it. Why should I be the one to get het up?

[*She stomps back down the beach and re-opens the chair, etc.*]

This is supposed to be a lesson, I'll give you a bloody lesson. You can use the money you stole, and your ice cream money, to go down to Mr Williams and buy me some lunch. Go on, Smarty Pants, get cracking. I know you can point to a salad roll.

[BILL *moves a couple of paces away.*]

Nothing like a practical demonstration, as they say in that fabulous book. Go on, I know you can point. And don't dawdle.

[*With that* MOLLY *slams herself down on the chair*

so hard that it upturns and she tumbles back with it, legs flying in the air.]

Wooooaaaa!

[BILL *turns and looks at her.*]

Billy! Billy!

[*He walks toward her and stops. There is no movement from* MOLLY. *Silence.*]

BILL: There was once this fox and this chicken . . .

[*The music swells as the gulls rise from behind the dune, swoop across the stage and fly off as the lights fade.* BILL *remains on stage. The music quietens as the lights rise on the house.* BILL *puts on a black arm band.* FRANCES *is sitting. The car horn is heard, then* DAN'*s voice calling to* BILL.]

DAN: Get out of the car, Billy.

[*He enters.*]

How about I shout the three of us to lunch at the pub?

FRANCES: Half the mourners will be there, pie-eyed. Do you really want to face that?

DAN: Whatever you think.

FRANCES: Thanks for coming down.

DAN: Got any cold beer?

FRANCES: Yes. [*Taking off her shoes*] The cool change was due two hours ago. Seems the weather man is about as reliable as the damned weather.

[*A car horn is heard.*]

DAN: Get out of the car, Billy. He's in a bitch of a mood.

FRANCES: Of course he is. We're all a bit —

[*The car horn sounds.*]

You won't be told again, get out of the car.

[BILL *walks to the top of the dune.*]

DAN: Share it?

[FRANCES *shakes her head, no.*]

You going to the library?

FRANCES: Should I?

DAN: Could take the afternoon off.

FRANCES: And leave Jan to — ?

DAN: The place won't fall apart.

FRANCES: No, but . . .

DAN: What?

FRANCES: Even the weather was the same. She was standing on the other side of the grave at Dad's funeral,
clutching onto Billy's hand. We hadn't seen each other
for ten years and she wouldn't look at me. That same
hot wind.

DAN: The beer'll cool you.

FRANCES: There had been no room in her life for anyone
else but Bill. Her whole world revolved around this
thing that did nothing but sit. She never shutting up,
Dad never accepting how he was. I'd eat my meals in
my room just to get away. I wished . . . I —

DAN: Go on.

FRANCES: I wished he had been killed.

[BILL *turns and looks at her.*]

FRANCES: I didn't care . . .

DAN: But you do.

FRANCES: Not then. I was driven out and my father to his
grave. This afternoon I, I'm so tired.

[*She sees* BILL *standing at the door.*]

Come in, Billy, you don't have to stand out there.

[*She eyes* DAN *as if she has been betrayed, then speaks
in a totally collected manner.*]

Go change out of your good clothes. Have a beer if you
want.

[BILL *shakes his head, no.*]

DAN: Want an ice cream?

[*He nods his head, yes.*]

There you go.

[*He holds out some money.* BILL *walks to collect it.*]

Keep the change.

[BILL *goes to leave.*]

FRANCES: Have lunch first, before you fill your face with
muck.

[*He stops and goes to the kitchen.*]

And take that arm band off. Funeral's over now.

[BILL *moves toward the bedroom.* DAN *stops him
gently.*]

DAN: Don't worry about it now, off you go. We've got a

couple of things to talk over.

[BILL *looks up at him, then to* FRANCES, *who avoids him.*]

FRANCES: Nothing that can't be said in front of him.

DAN: Oh?

FRANCES: Come here, and I'll undo the arm band.

[BILL *goes to move off;* DAN *holds his arm.*]

DAN: If you nick off now I'll give you an extra fifty cents for a double header.

[DAN *hands him the extra money.* BILL *goes to exit.*]

FRANCES: Stop it. Just what are you trying to do?

[BILL *stops.*]

DAN: Making sure you really want him to stay.

[FRANCES *is thrown by* DAN'*s reply, but adamantly sticks to her line of thinking.*]

FRANCES: Give back the money.

[BILL *goes over and hands* DAN *the money.*]

DAN: Forget it.

[BILL *puts the money back in his pocket and goes to exit.*]

FRANCES: He won't eat his lunch. Give it back.

DAN: Forget it.

FRANCES: Give it back.

[FRANCES *goes toward* BILL *and tries to take the money from his hand but* BILL *has already turned about and hurled it at the floor. He storms out of the house and onto the beach.*]

Come here, Billy, come back. Why did you do that?

DAN: What difference does an ice cream make? That's all it really amounts to.

FRANCES: How long was he standing there?

DAN: Let him go.

FRANCES: It's so easy for you to breeze in here . . .

DAN: It needn't have been like that.

FRANCES: [*moving away from him*] God, I wish that cool change would hurry up . . .

DAN: Do you really think you'll be able to cope without Molly feeding him, coming in every day, giving him lessons, making sure he doesn't wreck the joint?

FRANCES: She helped out because it gave her something to do. I can handle —

DAN: Nothing. With the best of intentions, you can handle nothing. Look what happened now.

FRANCES: You confused him. You come in here, throw your money about —

DAN: Oh, God.

FRANCES: I have to live with it twenty-four hours a day and yet you think you can come in here and tell me how to run my life and his.

DAN: You let that kid . . .

FRANCES: He is not a kid.

DAN: That's how you're treating him.

FRANCES: You had the chance to share our life and you chose not to. I respected that decision. Have the decency to respect mine.

DAN: Why are you shutting out the rest of the world? You're scared of letting him go.

FRANCES: If Joanna were like Bill, would you desert her?

DAN: I'd do what was best for both of us and I wouldn't call it desertion. I'm entitled to a life as well and I don't feel guilty about that.

FRANCES: Well, I would and I can't help how I feel. For years I ran away, dreading the prospect of ever facing him again. I made a decision . . .

DAN: But you can change that. He can't. You're not only denying yourself any sort of decent life, you're denying him one too.

FRANCES: Is it wrong to care?

DAN: No, but Christ Almighty, can't you see you're going backward?

FRANCES: He needs me.

DAN: You need him.

FRANCES: No.

DAN: You ran away then and you're still running . . .

FRANCES: No.

DAN: Dragging that man along as an excuse. You clutch onto him, frightened that one day he'll be gone too and what will you be left with then?

[*She moves away. He grabs her arm, she knocks it away.*]

Tell me, I have a right to know.

FRANCES: You have no rights.

DAN: We could have married.

FRANCES: Never.

DAN: You fucked up our life now you're doing the same to him. At least have the guts to let him go.

FRANCES: If it weren't for you he wouldn't be like he is.

BILL: [*Covering his ears and screaming*] No!

[*The lights go blue, except around* BILL. DAN *and* FRANCES *are caught in this moment.*]

I ran from the back door. Our house was filled with voices. Something . . . was happening. I didn't stop. I tore, raced, ran breathless to the beach. As I reached this spot, I looked back and saw them . . . through the window. I can see them in the house. He was waving his arms about. She turned. Screamed at him. I had seen that look of hate before. A face about to crack open. I understood what she was talking about. I understand. Here. Now.

[*Music begins as the gulls swoop on and settle before him. He shoos them away with his hand.*]

Go away. There's nothing for you today. Your bread's back at the house.

[*They settle near his feet.*]

Didn't you hear me? Go over to Mrs Dwyer's, she's not there any more, or out front. Try aiming for that Holden sedan parked there.

[*A gull comes toward him.*]

Didn't you hear . . ?

[*It flutters up unsteadily and settles again. It appears to be sickly.*]

What's the matter?

[*He reaches his hand out to the gull.*]

What's wrong?

[*The other gull flies in the air and swoops at the sick one, slightly knocking him.*]

Leave him.

[BILL *tries to coax the sick one toward him.*]

Here . . . come here. I won't harm you.

[*The sick gull tries to move away but* BILL *grabs it. It flutters helplessly in his hand.*]

What's happened to you? Don't fight.

[*The other gull swoops at* BILL.]

Get away. I'm not going to . . . harm him.

[*He looks at the sick gull then addresses the other.*]

It's all right for you to fly about in the sky all day. If I could do that I wouldn't be such a worry to Frances. Oh, we could go . . . wherever we wanted . . . swooping and diving into the sea . . . bliss . . . she'd know I was just about the cliffs with you boys. No.

[*He throws the gull from his hand and it flutters unsteadily.*]

No more. Get away. Both of you. Fly . . . fly while you can. Our time . . . has run out.

[*The gulls fly off.*]

You've got to believe me . . . I don't mean to be any trouble . . .

[*The lights come back to normal.*]

DAN: You blame me?

[FRANCES *says nothing.*]

Have you always blamed me? [*Demanding an answer*] Blamed me all this time. Answer me, please.

FRANCES: Blame you . . . yes . . . and him. I'm sorry.

[*She exits.* DAN *gets up, puts on his jacket to go.* FRANCES *re-enters with* BILL'*s lunch things and a new bottle of beer.*]

Billy. Lunch.

DAN: Did you ever love me?

FRANCES: I never . . . couldn't love you as much . . . but I still needed you. Desperately needed you. Was that selfish of me? Hold me, Dan. I'm so tired. Hold me.

DAN: It's destroying you.

FRANCES: [*trying to break away*] No.

DAN: Destroying you as it did me —

FRANCES: Where is he?

DAN: It almost killed me —

FRANCES: He shouldn't be out in the sun.

DAN: Frances, listen. For years I almost let it kill me . . .

FRANCES: You're hurting me.

DAN: I was so bound up with the guilt of it all —

FRANCES: Billy —

DAN: That I had no real life. I allowed it to eat away at myself.

FRANCES: Billy!

DAN: It will —

FRANCES: Billy!

DAN: . . . destroy you. Frances, it will destroy —

[BILL *has rushed up from the beach. He pulls* FRANCES *away from* DAN, *protecting her, then attacks* DAN.]

Billy, calm down. Let me explain.

[*A short fight ensues in which* DAN *gets punched several times. The chairs are knocked over, etc.*]

FRANCES: Stop it, stop hitting him . . .

[*The scuffle continues till* BILL *grabs the beer bottle, smashing it and threatening* DAN.]

No! Put it down. Down.

[BILL *does so.*]

Go to your room. Go on.

DAN: Let him stay. Bill . . .

FRANCES: Go to your room.

DAN: Stay out of this.

[*He walks slowly to* BILL *and speaks in a very placatory manner, very aware of the bottle still near his hand.*]

Bill, I wasn't trying to hurt Frances. I would never do that. But no matter what goes on between the two of us, it really has nothing to do with you . . .

FRANCES: Billy . . .

[DAN *indicates to* FRANCES *that she should stay out of this argument, then continues to talk to* BILL.]

DAN: Nothing to do with you. Now I'm going to treat you as I would any bloke that did what you've just done to me. Fair enough?

[BILL *tries to speak as* DAN *punches him in the stomach.*]

FRANCES: No.

[*She tries to pull* DAN *off* BILL.]

DAN: Fair enough.

[*He punches him in the stomach again and* BILL *collapses to the floor.*]

We'll leave it at that, OK? Bye, Bill.

[DAN *exits.*]

FRANCES: What has he done to you . . . oh what has he done to you?

[*She goes over to him but* BILL *shies away.*]

I want to help you — What's the matter?

[*She gets no response from* BILL.]

Is it Dan and me? Do you think I've lied to you? You're being too hard on me, Billy. You wouldn't have understood.

[*He turns to her.*]

I did it to protect you. It's all gone wrong, Billy . . . all wrong.

[*She moves to him again but he shies away.*]

Oh, make him understand . . . He asked me to marry, but you would've had to go . . . Thank God . . . Oh, thank God I knew I made the right decision. I'll never let you down.

[*She goes to him.*]

We'll start again.

[*He starts to make his lunch.*]

Just the two of us. We are not a lost cause. No. It's them. I'll never leave you again. From now on it's just going to be us.

[*He takes hold of her hands and releases himself.*]

BILL: I'm going off to play with my mates.

[*He smiles and touches her face.*]

I love you . . .

[*As* BILL *gets up and goes down to the beach the lights on the house fade. For the first time the actual cry of the gulls is heard.* BILL *falls to his knees and looks skyward. A single gull flies down, swooping des-*

perately from side to side.]

And in the morning, as the gulls fly up . . .

[*The gull's crying intensifies to screaming pitch as it flies frenetically, dipping and rising as* BILL *takes the jagged bottle from his pocket, raises it, and slashes his throat from ear to ear. The gull does one last sweep across the beach. The crying fades and the music once again comes back to its melodic self. The gull flies as high as it can go, wings fully extended. Freeze. The lights fade to black.*]

THE END